ORGANIZED CHAOS

by

Brandon S. Todd

Brandon S. Todd
820 North Flint St.
Lincolnton, NC 28092
704-501-6135
brandonstodd@abbey.bac.edu

Order this book online at www.trafford.com
or email orders@trafford.com

Most Trafford titles are also available at major online book retailers.

Print information available on the last page.

ISBN: 978-1-4907-7862-4 (sc)
ISBN: 978-1-4907-7863-1 (e)

Library of Congress Control Number: 2016918764

Trafford rev. 12/1/2016

Trafford
PUBLISHING®   www.trafford.com
North America & international
toll-free: 1 888 232 4444 (USA & Canada)
fax: 812 355 4082

FADE IN:

INT. RESTAURANT - DAY

                                    YEAR: 2012

LOS ANGELES: A Red Lobster-like RESTAURANT. The RESTAURANT
is filled with many people. In the very back of the
RESTAURANT are THREE MEN; one is white (MICHAEL CARTER), one
is black (DRE FERRARA), one is bi-racial (MICKEY MONTANA).
The THREE MEN are each in their early 30's.

The THREE MEN are wearing casual clothing. They are dressed
in an unassuming fashion...

They are trying not to draw attention to themselves...

Each of them is drinking a STELLA ARTOIS. They are talking
over their finished dinner...

                    MICKEY
          I'm going to Amsterdam. That's my
          ultimate dream...I wanna smoke
          that Amsterdam bud until the sun
          goes down, and then comes back up.
          No stress, no worries, just pure
          relaxation.

                    DRE
               (in agreement)
          That sounds like a plan.

                    CARTER
               (shaking his head
                in disagreement)
          Nah. The Caribbean is where it's
          at, man. Fine women, nice beaches,
          you name it. You haven't lived
          until you've lived by that
          Caribbean water.

                    MICKEY
               (laughing
                uncontrollably)
          Listen to CARTER over here,
          sounding like a fucking salesman.
          Man, take that shit on the arches.

                    CARTER
          It's the truth, and you know it.

                    DRE
               (responding to
               CARTER)
          All I know is, that pussy you've
          been eating has gone to your brain
          and now it's coming out of your
          mouth. Fuck the Caribbean, man;
          there's too much going on in
          places like that. It's too easy to
          get spotted. Like Mickey, I like
          the quiet, reserved spots where
          you can just chill, ponder and
          most of all, blend in.

                    CARTER
          Fuck it. When we're retired I'll
          go to the Caribbean, and you guys
          can fuck off somewhere else.

                    MICKEY
          All right, like I said, I'm going
          to Amsterdam; no ifs, ands, or
          buts about it. Besides, when we're
          done you won't need us, and we
          damn sure won't need you. And,
          when you go to the Caribbean
          you'll get pinched faster than a
          zit.

                    CARTER
               (being facetious)
          Uh-huh. I'm still going to the
          Caribbean. And, you guys should go
          with me. You boys couldn't tie
          your shoes without me around. I'm
          the real leader of this team...I'm
          MJ, you guys are Pippen and
          Rodman.

                    MICKEY
               (condescending)
          That'll be the day. You are more
          useless than tits on a boar-hog,
          CARTER.

                    CARTER
          Yeah, whatever. Anyways, you guys
          watch the game last night?

                                   CUT TO:

MICKEY shakes his head in disgust.

                         DRE
          Yeah, I checked it out. I didn't
          see it all, but I caught the
          highlights this morning. The Heat
          took it. Lebron has finally
          cemented himself as an NBA legend.

MICKEY becomes wide-eyed and obviously angered. He is a
beautiful monster...

MICKEY has hair like that of a lion's mane. His hair is
shiny and black. He has no facial hair.

He has khaki skin, yet his pigmentation has a distinct
paleness to it. He is bi-racial. He is a hybrid of the black
and white races...

His eyes are as dark as dark-matter.

He is a Man filled with passion, pride, and prejudice.

MICKEY MONTANA is a lost soul, with a lost purpose; he's a
rebel without a cause. He is filled with contempt and
conviction...

MICKEY is a Man of Greed, Lust, Envy, Wrath, Pride,
Gluttony, and Sloth. He is a Man of Sin...

                         MICKEY
                    (with great apathy
                     and aversion)
          Fuck the NBA, man. It's all
          rigged, that's the real sport.
          And, the blacks have taken over
          the whole damn league anyway.
          Whatever happened to fundamentals?
          Whatever happened to Pistol Pete,
          Bill Lambier, Bill Walton, John
          Stockton, and even Larry Bird? You
          can't turn on an NBA game without
          seeing a bunch of 7 ft black guys,
          that can't even read, who can't
          shoot, pass, or play, running
          around in baggy ass uniforms
          looking like race-horses chasing
          after an apple.

                         CARTER
          There are still plenty of whites
          in the league, MICKEY.

DRE and CARTER are just sipping their beers.

MICKEY quickly chugs the rest of his STELLA ARTOIS and sits the empty bottle to the side.

He has two more fresh beers sitting to the side of his dinner-plate, as do DRE and CARTER.

MICKEY pops the top of another beer, but he waits to take a drink.

                    MICKEY
               (with a fire in
                his eyes)
          Yeah, CARTER, true. But, most of
          the whites playing in the league
          today, that are good, are mostly
          all European...
               (wholeheartedly)
          ...My primary point is, that
          blacks are taking over everything,
          and they're ruining this
          God-forsaken nation...

                    DRE
               (defensively)
          Hey, MICKEY, chill the fuck out,
          man, this isn't the 60's; you
          can't just be slinging the word
          "blacks" around. Have some fucking
          decency.

                    MICKEY
          Decency? Fuck you, and fuck
          decency...

                    DRE
               (pissed by
                MICKEY'S remarks)
          Plus, you're half black, man, what
          the hell is your deal?

                    MICKEY
          Yeah, I'm half black, so what? I
          still hate black people, with the
          exception of you, DRE.

                    DRE
               (questioning)
          But, why?

                    MICKEY
          I've got my list of reasons. Let's
          just leave it at that, all right.

                    CARTER
                (confused)
        I always here you talking about
        black people, yet you're the one
        who chose to wear the
        OBAMA-MASK...

                    MICKEY
        Hey, I'm a man of irony. What more
        can I say?

                    DRE
                (challenging
                MICKEY)
        You're a racist and a psychopath,
        that's what you are, brother.

                                        CUT TO:

MICKEY looks at his two accomplices with a passionate look;
passionate, yet honest and truly uncompromising.

                    MICKEY
                (very serious and
                 with power)
        The world needs people like me;
        like us. We organize true CHAOS...
                (smiles gleefully)
        ...Who's gonna stop us???

                    CARTER
                (in agreement)
        He's right, DRE. Without people
        like MICKEY, and like us, the
        world would be too organized.
        Without people like us The World
        would be too civil. If everyone
        obeys every law, and complies to
        every authority around them, then,
        eventually, people speak less,
        express less, and are oppressed
        more...

                                        CUT TO:

MICKEY slaps his hand on the table.

                    MICKEY
                (raises voice)
        Our criminality makes civility
        possible. We are needed in this
        society, so people can say there's
        the bad guy, right there!

                  CARTER
      But, who's to say we're the
      criminals?

                              CUT TO:

MICKEY is a Byronic-bastard. He chugs all of the beer in a
few seconds and retorts.

                  MICKEY
         (with great
          conviction)
      What is wrong is wrong. We steal,
      and that's wrong; that's criminal.
      But, who we steal from justifies
      our actions. We will be portrayed
      as villains, right now, in the
      moment, but, in reality, we are
      the heroes. For the time being
      I'll take being the villain, but
      when the whole goddamn system
      collapses...who will they look up
      to then?

MICKEY grabs another STELLA ARTOIS and pops the top.

                   DRE
      Hey, I don't disagree one bit.
      Somebody has to be the villains.
      Why not us?

                  MICKEY
      Exactly...

The THREE MEN raise their beers in a toast.

                  MICKEY
        (raising his beer)
      To the next job.

                       FADE TO BLACK:

                       CHAPTER TITLE
                       APPEARANCE:

I. GRAPE SODA, CIGARETTES AND BEER

                       FADE IN:

EXT. HOUSE - MORNING

Two MEN pull up to a HOUSE in a 2012 YELLOW CHEVY CAMARO.

The MEN exit the 2012 YELLOW CHEVY CAMARO.

The MEN are GERALD NIXON and VITO TEDESCO. GERALD is black.
He exits the driver-side of the VEHICLE. VITO is white. He
exits the passenger-side of the VEHICLE. Both are in their
mid-40's, and both are wearing suits; a black blazer, black
slacks, and white button-up shirts.

The men's outfits match with the exception of their ties;
GERALD is wearing a solid-red tie, and VITO is wearing a
royal-blue tie...

They walk up to the front-door of the HOUSE. They knock and
a WOMAN comes to the door, but she doesn't open it
immediately...

                    JACKIE
               (nervously)
          Who is it?

                    VITO
          We are Federal Agents, ma'am. Open
          the door.

                    JACKIE
          Yes, one minute, please...

The MEN patiently wait for the door to open.

The WOMAN finally opens the door about 20 seconds later. She
is as nervous as a alleycat in bathwater. The two MEN pull
badges from the interior-pockets of their jackets and they
flash the badges quick as lightning.

                    VITO
          JACKIE JAMES, my name is
          special-agent TEDESCO. This is my
          partner...
               (points thumb at
               GERALD)
          ...special-agent NIXON. We have a
          couple of questions to ask you
          regarding your son. May we come
          in?

                    JACKIE
          Yes, sir, p-p-please, come on in.

                              CUT TO:

The MEN walk into the HOUSE.

                                        CUT TO:

INT. HOUSE - MOMENTS LATER

GERALD and VITO examine the interior of the HOUSE as they
enter.

                    GERALD
          This is a nice little setup you
          got here...I like the interior
          design. Did you do it yourself?

                    JACKIE
          Yes, I did it myself. What do you
          want with my son???

                    GERALD
               (stomps the floor
                hard as hell)
          Is this ceramic tile?

                    JACKIE
          Y-y-yeah, it is, sir.

                    GERALD
          Damn, it's quite nice. I like it a
          lot, ma'am.

                    JACKIE
               (with sass)
          Are you here to question me about
          my son, or check out the interior
          design of my home?

                    GERALD
          I apologize, ma'am. Let me allow
          my partner to fill you in on the
          situation.

                    VITO
          Well, Miss JAMES. Your son is in
          trouble with some very powerful
          people. We need JASON to come in
          for questioning. He allegedly
          robbed some people, and
          subsequently murdered them. Now,
          we don't know if it's him who
          committed the crime, for sure, but
          if he's here or if you know where
          we can find him, it would be best
          to tell us so we can resolve this
                    (MORE)

                    VITO (cont'd)
matter peacefully, and restore his
innocence...

                    JACKIE
                (nervously)
I honestly don't know where he is.
I haven't seen him in weeks, nor
have I talked to him.

                    GERALD
                (politely)
May we have a seat, ma'am?

                    JACKIE
Yes, go ahead.

                    VITO
Thank you.

The two MEN take a seat on the couch in the living-room of
the HOUSE.

                    GERALD
Would you mind if I had a drink?

                    JACKIE
Yes, you may. What would you like?
We have grape soda, sweet tea,
milk, and beer.

                    GERALD
I'll take a glass of grape soda...

                    JACKIE
All right, I'll go fix you a
glass. Anything for you, agent
TEDESCO?

                    VITO
No, thank you, ma'am. However, may
I light a cigarette in here?

                    JACKIE
Of course.

VITO searches his pockets for a lighter, seemingly not able
to find one.

                    VITO
I think I've lost my lighter. Do
you have one?

                         JACKIE
          No, I don't, sorry. I don't--

She doesn't finish her sentence. She looks very nervous.

                         VITO
          --Oh, it's no big deal, I found
          mine.

VITO pulls out a black lighter.

                         JACKIE
          I'll get you an ash-tray.

JACKIE gets an ash-tray for VITO; the ash-tray is filled
with cigarette butts. Subsequently she walks into the
kitchen to get a glass of grape soda for GERALD. As she is
in the kitchen fixing the drink, GERALD and VITO stay seated
on the couch and look around the den with their eyes wide.

JACKIE comes back into the living-room from the kitchen.
VITO lights up his cigarette as soon as JACKIE gives GERALD
his drink.

                         VITO
                    (puffing his
                     cigarette)
          So, Miss JAMES, do you remember
          exactly the last time you saw your
          son?

                         JACKIE
                    (evasively)
          No, I cannot. I do know that it
          was about 3 weeks ago, but I can't
          say exactly when I saw him.

                         GERALD
          Do you live here by yourself?

                         JACKIE
          Yes, my husband passed two years
          back, and my son moved out about a
          year ago. So, yes, I do live here
          alone.

GERALD chugs his drink quickly.

VITO takes a long puff off of his cigarette.

JACKIE looks confused and somewhat intimidated.

                    GERALD
        I thank you for the drink, ma'am.
        I do have one question, though.

                    JACKIE
        Yes, agent NIXON?

                    GERALD
        What is a woman like you doing
        smoking cigarettes, and drinking
        beer and grape soda?

JACKIE responds nervously.

                    JACKIE
        I smoke occasionally, I like grape
        soda, and I drink beer every now
        and then. So, what? Is that a
        crime, sir?

                    GERALD
        No, of course not. It's just that
        we've been here for several
        minutes, and you have yet to light
        a cigarette. Do you know what that
        tells us?

                    JACKIE
        What's that?

                    VITO
            (puts his
             cigarette down
             and lets it burn)
        Someone else is here...

                    JACKIE
            (nervously)
        No. No one else is here. No one
        is here, it's just me.

                    GERALD
            (assertive)
        If you were a smoker then you
        would be smoking right now. Your
        ash-tray is full and that tells me
        you're at least a pack a day
        smoker. A pack a day smoker would
        have already went through two
        cigarettes by now. You are not a
        smoker, and you do not drink grape
        soda or beer. But, I'm sure your
        son does, huh? Tell me
        something...how did you manage to
                    (MORE)

                    GERALD (cont'd)
        hide him in the wall there?

                    JACKIE
                 (in great fear)
        What?! No, please!!! Don't hurt my
        son!!! He didn't do anything!

GERALD and VITO stand up from the couch and they draw
pistols.

                    GERALD
                 (drawing his
                  weapon)
        We're not here to judge, we're
        here to punish!

GERALD shoots JACKIE in the head...

Subsequently, GERALD and VITO unload their clips at the wall
across from them. A body is heard dropping and a man, JASON,
is heard crying out in pain.

                    JASON
        Ahhh! Ahhh!

JASON squeals like a stuck-pig, lets out a final breath and
dies.

GERALD examines the wall for an entry way into the hiding
spot in the wall.

GERALD finds a slight crease in the wall. He fiddles with
the crease in the wall and a door opens. GERALD pulls out a
flashlight and looks inside the hiding place; he identifies
the body as JASON JAMES.

                    VITO
                 (picks his
                  cigarette back up)
        Did we get him?

                    GERALD
        Yeah, we got him. Now, let's peel
        and give BRODY the news.

                    VITO
                 (puffs his
                  cigarette a few
                  more times)
        All right, let's do it.

VITO puffs his cigarette one last time, and then puts it out
in the ash-tray.

                    GERALD
                (growing impatient)
          Come on, nigga, get that shit put
          out, let's go! We ain't got all
          day!

                    VITO
          Okay, man, my fault. Shit.

GERALD and VITO exit the HOUSE.

                                        CUT TO:

EXT. HOUSE - MOMENTS LATER

VITO and GERALD walk to the 2012 YELLOW CAMARO.

                    VITO
          I didn't think she'd buy that
          "Agent"-line.

                    GERALD
          Hell, me either.

The two MEN enter the 2012 YELLOW CHEVY CAMARO. GERALD is
driving. He and VITO ride off from the HOUSE.

                                        FADE TO BLACK:

                                        CHAPTER TITLE
                                        APPEARANCE:

II. THE ELITE

                                        CUT TO:

                                        FADE IN:

EXT. CITY STREET - DAY

Four MEN are zooming down a CITY STREET in an AMBULANCE with
the AMBULANCE-siren flashing and blaring.

                                        CUT TO:

INT. AMBULANCE - CONTINUOUS

In the AMBULANCE are MICKEY, DRE, and CARTER all dressed up
in formal PRESIDENTIAL attire; they are wearing very
fashionable business suits, with matching black-leather
gloves, and matching American-flag-themed ties.

                              CUT TO:

MICKEY, DRE, and CARTER also have on MASKS...

The MASKS resemble that of President Barack Obama(MICKEY),
President George W. Bush(CARTER), and President Bill
Clinton(DRE): these are the MASKS that 'THE ELITE' wear
while committing robberies.

The fourth MAN in the AMBULANCE is in the disguise of a
paramedic and he is THE DRIVER.

                              CUT TO:

'THE ELITE' are riding along in the back of the AMBULANCE,
readying machine-guns while also talking to one another
using accents mimicking those of their masked disguises, in
a role-playing manner.

                    OBAMA-MASK
               (in a playful
               manner)
          All right, Mr. Clinton, you and I
          will control the crowd. Mr. Bush,
          you gather and secure the loot...

                    GEORGE-MASK
          No problem, Mr. President. Let's
          do this...

                    BILL-MASK
          Whenever you're ready, Mr.
          President!

The DRIVER turns off the AMBULANCE-siren as they near a
BANK.

                              CUT TO:

The MEN arrive at the BANK in the AMBULANCE.

MICKEY kicks open the AMBULANCE doors, and he, DRE, and
CARTER exit the AMBULANCE with their guns in-hand. They are
each carrying a duffle bag...

                         OBAMA-MASK
                    (commando-style)
              Let's go!

                         GEORGE-MASK
              Yes, sir, Mr. President!

                                             CUT TO:

EXT. BANK - MOMENTS LATER

MICKEY, DRE, and CARTER slowly walk up the BANK stairs in a
militant fashion. They rush through the BANK doors.

                                             CUT TO:

INT. BANK - MOMENTS LATER

MICKEY, DRE, and CARTER each shoot a few rounds at the
ceiling of the BANK, and they proceed to dominate the crowd.

                         OBAMA-MASK
                    (In a manic tone)
              Good day, ladies and gentlemen! We
              are THE ELITE! We only need a few
              minutes of your time and a few of
              the BANK'S dollars and we'll be
              out of your way. If any of you try
              anything I'll put a bullet in each
              and every last one of ya!

                         BILL-MASK
              Everyone be cool, this is a
              robbery! Put your hands on your
              heads and faces on the ground, and
              we won't have any problems!

The crowd in the bank comply and get on the ground with
their hands on their heads and their faces on the ground.
The robbers are recklessly pointing their weapons at the
civilians and employees, greatly intimidating them.

                         GEORGE-MASK
                    (giggling)
              This is a matter of
              national-security, folks. Any of
              you want to be brave and hit the
              alarm, I won't mind pulling this
              trigger. You're all Terrorists!

CARTER fires several more rounds at the ceiling of the BANK.

                        OBAMA-MASK
            As you all know, I am your
            president. We came here for the
            BANK'S money only, so cooperate
            and no one will get hurt. That, I
            can assure you. If you are
            uncooperative, then I can also
            assure you that you will be on the
            fast track to heaven.

MICKEY and DRE hand their duffle bags to CARTER...

                        OBAMA-MASK
            Now, Mr. Bush, please grab that
            manager and make him open the
            SAFE. If he resists, break his
            face...

                        GEORGE-MASK
            Certainly, Mr. President!

CARTER grabs the BANK MANAGER and walks him to the SAFE
while pointing his weapon to the back of the BANK MANAGER'S
head.

                        GEORGE-MASK
            Open the safe! NOW!

                        BANK-MANAGER
                (frantic)
            OK! Please, p-p-please don't hurt
            me!

                        GEORGE-MASK
                (angered)
            Just open the SAFE, pal! Or I'll
            bust your skull open!

The BANK MANAGER opens the SAFE. CARTER enters the SAFE with
the three duffel bags.

                                        CUT TO:

INT. SAFE - MOMENTS LATER

In the SAFE lies at least $950,000 in cold-hard-cash,
unwrapped, stacked and without dye-packs. Also, in the SAFE
there is a black BRIEFCASE. CARTER begins loading the
cash-loot into the three duffel bags.

                        GEORGE-MASK
            Damn!!

                                        CUT TO:

INT. BANK - CONTINUOUS

As CARTER places the cash into the duffel bags, MICKEY and
DRE condescendingly speak to the crowd in a parody-like
manner. MICKEY and DRE are still pointing their machine-guns
at the people in the in the BANK...

                    OBAMA-MASK
                (yelling in a
                 manic tone)
            We need change, folks! But we'll
            take all this money instead! It'll
            do!

                    BILL-MASK
                (looking at MICKEY)
            Mr. President, I think we have
            this situation under control, much
            like the nation! I commend your
            efforts!

                    OBAMA-MASK
            Very much so, Mr. Clinton! Mr.
            Bush should be done any moment
            now!

                                        CUT TO:

INT. SAFE - MOMENTS LATER

CARTER has the money loaded up and brings the duffel bags
out one at a time. After getting the third bag, CARTER grabs
the BRIEFCASE and then exits the SAFE.

                                        CUT TO:

INT. BANK - MOMENTS LATER

MICKEY continues to point his weapon at the crowd.

DRE and CARTER each have a duffel bag and head toward the
BANK doors.

CARTER leaves a bag and the BRIEFCASE in the BANK for MICKEY
to get.

                                        CUT TO:

EXT. BANK - MOMENTS LATER

DRE and CARTER are walking quickly down the steps to the
AMBULANCE.

                    BILL-MASK
                 (concerned)
          What the fuck is MICKEY doing? We
          don't have any time to kill! He
          needs to hurry it up and quit
          showing off before the pigs show
          up, man!

                    GEORGE-MASK
          Don't worry about him, he knows
          exactly what he's doing. He loves
          being theatrical. You know that.
          Leave him be, no pigs are going to
          get us on this job, let the man
          work. Besides, he is the
          president...

CARTER and DRE load the two duffel bags into the AMBULANCE,
and they hop inside the AMBULANCE...

One bag is left to be got inside the BANK, along with the
mysterious BRIEFCASE...

                                        CUT TO:

INT. BANK - MOMENTS LATER

MICKEY still pointing his weapon at the crowd, grabs the
last duffel bag full of cash and the BRIEFCASE. Before
exiting the BANK he speaks facetiously to the crowd.

                    MICKEY
                 (being facetious)
          Everyone, it has been my great
          pleasure to stimulate the economy
          this evening! Oh, and, by the way,
          please don't forget to vote; it's
          the most you can do!

MICKEY looks at one of the BANK cameras. He doesn't shoot
it. He just looks at it. He is that arrogant.

MICKEY then exits the BANK with the duffel bag and the
BRIEFCASE, laughing like a lunatic.

                                        CUT TO:

EXT. BANK - MOMENTS LATER

MICKEY walks down the BANK stairs toward the AMBULANCE. He enters the AMBULANCE and 'THE ELITE' take off from the scene of CHAOS.

'THE ELITE' move like The Devil...

                                        CUT TO:

INT. AMBULANCE - MOMENTS LATER

MICKEY, DRE, and CARTER remove their MASKS...

                    MICKEY
          Those fuckers make it so easy!

                                        CUT TO:

EXT. CITY STREET - CONTINUOUS

Police-sirens can be heard in the distance, but the Police are too far off to stop 'THE ELITE'. THE DRIVER is flooring it and he cuts the AMBULANCE-siren back on. Sirens are screaming throughout LA.

                                        CUT TO:

INT. AMBULANCE - MOMENTS LATER

MICKEY, DRE, and CARTER are organizing their things and the loot...

                    MICKEY
               (smirking)
          Now, that was a hell of a job
          boys. Clean, effective, and
          efficient; robbery at its finest.
          Let's clean ourselves up and I'll
          get this BRIEFCASE delivered to
          BRODY...

                                        CUT TO:

EXT. CITY STREET - MOMENTS LATER

THE DRIVER pulls into a PARKING COMPLEX.

                    MICKEY
               (commanding)
          Go to the 6th level...

                    THE DRIVER
               (agreeable)
          You got it, Boss...

                    MICKEY
               (pissed)
          I'm not your boss, fella...I am
          nobodies boss. You got me?

                    THE DRIVER
          Yes, Sir...

                    MICKEY
               (pointing at the
               DRIVER with his
               thumb)
          This fucking guy...

                                        CUT TO:

EXT. PARKING COMPLEX - MOMENTS LATER

THE DRIVER takes the AMBULANCE up all 5 levels and proceeds
to the 6th...

                                        CUT TO:

THE DRIVER parks the AMBULANCE on the 6th level. There are
some vehicles around, but there are no people on the 6th
level of the PARKING COMPLEX.

                                        CUT TO:

INT. AMBULANCE - CONTINUOUS

                    MICKEY
          All right, DRE, you go East.
          CARTER, you go West. I'll call you
          guys after I'm done meeting with
          BRODY.

                                        CUT TO:

DRE and CARTER nod their heads at the same time, with
understanding. They know the drill.

                                        CUT TO:

THE DRIVER looks at the three MEN quite bewildered.

                    THE DRIVER
              (confused and
               curious)
          Who the Hell is BRODY? What about
          me, guys? What about my cut?

MICKEY, DRE, and CARTER smirk at THE DRIVER.

                              CUT TO:

MICKEY pulls a blade so quickly that THE DRIVER can't even
blink before MICKEY plunges the blade into his temple.

                    THE DRIVER
              (convulsing)
          Aahhh!!!
              (bleeding from his
               eyes)
          Ahhh!!!

The DRIVER stops convulsing and dies.

Every DRIVER that works with THE ELITE gets whacked; it's
how they work. BRODY has the crew kill the DRIVER after
every job. MICKEY, DRE, and CARTER like it that way; they
are a tight crew and they would never let another on their
team or in on their schemes...

                              CUT TO:

EXT. PARKING COMPLEX - MOMENTS LATER

MICKEY, DRE, and CARTER hop out of the AMBULANCE with fresh
clothes on. DRE and CARTER rush off and proceed to leave the
PARKING COMPLEX with the cash-loot.

MICKEY stays behind with the BRIEFCASE...

                              CUT TO:

MICKEY grabs a can of gasoline that he has and pours the gas
all over THE DRIVER's body and the interior of the
AMBULANCE. He does so with great haste.

                              CUT TO:

MICKEY pulls a book of matches from his pocket. He strikes a
match and then tosses it into the AMBULANCE, setting the
vehicle ablaze. 'THE ELITE' leave no traces. They are
cleaner than "Mr. Clean".

                              CUT TO:

As The AMBULANCE burns, MICKEY walks away with a great big
smile on his face. He loves what he does. MICKEY MONTANA is
a man who wants to watch The World burn; he'd set it on fire
if he could...

                              CUT TO:

INT. TORTURE CHAMBER - EVENING

VITO and GERALD have kidnapped a SNITCH that was planning on
giving information to the FBI and CIA about BRODY.

BRODY is a King-Pin. He is a intimidating figure. BRODY is
big, tall, white, old, clean-shaven and bald, and he is THE
BOSS. Although he is old, he is still in great shape; he is
built like an NFL linebacker. BRODY is wearing a black
tank-top w/ suspenders, 'DeBo'-slippers, and fancy black
slacks. He has on a modest gold chain, and a gold ring on
his right middle finger...

BRODY dresses like a Boss and he rules like a God.

                              CUT TO:

BRODY, VITO, and GERALD are standing in a TORTURE CHAMBER,
smoking, waiting for THE SNITCH to gain consciousness.
GERALD and VITO are smoking joints. BRODY is smoking a
COHIBA.

THE SNITCH is strapped to a metal chair. His hands, arms,
feet, and legs are bound to the metal chair with
metallic-straps...

                              CUT TO:

THE SNITCH wakes up and starts yelling. He tries to get up
from the metal chair, but he is not able.

                         BRODY
                    (intimidatingly)
               Hello there...

                         THE SNITCH
                    (trembling with
                     fear)
               Oh, My God!!!

                         BRODY
               Yes, I might as well be your God,
               you little-snitch. You vermin...

THE SNITCH
P-p-please don't hurt me, sir!

VITO and GERALD chief their joints. BRODY places his cigar
in an ash-tray, and gets a sip of water...

                              CUT TO:

VITO, and GERALD toke their joints a little more and then
they put them down in the ash-tray. VITO and GERALD then
both put on black-latex gloves.

BRODY clears his throat and grips his suspenders...

                    BRODY
          You know, my grandfather taught me
          a tale that I'll never
          forget...allow me to tell you that
          tale.

                    THE SNITCH
          Yes, Sir! J-j-just please, BRODY,
          don't hurt me, man!!!

                    BRODY
          Okay. The tale goes as so:

          A guy named MIKE and his buddy
          CRAIG traveled around the World.
          As they were getting back to The
          Airport, preparing to go back to
          Georgia, MIKE runs into his old
          friend CHARLIE.

          Now, CHARLIE is glad to see MIKE.
          He asks, "How ya doing, MIKE?".

          MIKE says, "Well, I'm great. CRAIG
          and I just got through traveling
          the World."

          CHARLIE was excited to hear about
          the trip and he was curious as to
          where CRAIG was: "Where is CRAIG?"
          Charlie asked. "Aah. He's still in
          the back of The Airport. He
          doesn't get around so good. He's
          crippled, you know?" replied
          MIKE...

          CHARLIE didn't expect to hear such
          bad news: "Oh, I didn't know."

          He still wanted to hear about The
                    (MORE)

BRODY (cont'd)

Trip..."So, how was your trip?"
asked CHARLIE.

"Great" said MIKE. He continued on
saying, "CRAIG and I went to New
York, London, and Italy."

"Awesome" remarked CHARLIE.

MIKE kept rambling. "While in New
York, I went to The Statue of
Liberty."

CHARLIE stopped MIKE, and asked
"Well, what about CRAIG?"

MIKE replied: "Ah. He couldn't
walk up it. He's crippled, you
know."

"Damn" said CHARLIE.

"Next, I went to see BIG BEN, in
London..."

"Wow!" said CHARLIE.

"Well, what about CRAIG?" asked
CHARLIE.

MIKE replied: "Ah. He stayed at
The Hotel, he's crippled, you
know."

"Man, that's terrible." responded
CHARLIE.

"Yep." said MIKE.

"Anyway, next we went to Italy. We
were right outside of The Vatican.
It was beautiful. And, The Pope,
himself, came out of The Vatican."
said MIKE, with great excitement.

"Oh, Man, that's amazing!"
responded CHARLIE.

"Yep." said MIKE.

"...And, when The Pope appeared,
he looked directly at CRAIG, and
I, and he walked right up to
(MORE)

                         BRODY (cont'd)
          CRAIG, and he told him to "Rise
          and Walk". Suddenly, CRAIG stood
          up from his wheel-chair with his
          crutches. The Pope blessed him,
          and one of his crutches flew off
          into the wind. The Pope blessed
          him again, and his other crutch
          went flying off in the wind..."
          explained MIKE.

          CHARLIE was curious, and he asked:
          "Well, CRAIG walked, right?!"

          MIKE responded: "Nah, he busted
          his ass. He's crippled, you know."

THE SNITCH is actually calmed down a little-bit. BRODY'S
voice is actually kind of soothing.

THE SNITCH even lets out a slight giggle at the joke.

                         BRODY
          Do you want to know the moral of
          that tale?

THE SNITCH sits dazed, but nods his head in a yes-manner.

                         BRODY
          The moral is that this World is
          going to Hell, and so is everybody
          and everything in it.

BRODY gives a go-ahead to GERALD.

GERALD grabs a syringe, with a very long needle. The shot is
filled with a customized paralysis-agent. GERALD injects THE
SNITCH in the neck; the shot paralyses THE SNITCH while
still allowing him to feel pain.

BRODY then gives a go-ahead to VITO.

VITO walks to the other side of the room, and he grabs a
black-box. He opens the box, and in it is a Mason-Jar full
of countless fire-ants.

                         BRODY
                    (to THE SNITCH)
          Prepare to feel Hell...

BRODY nods at VITO.

VITO walks up to THE SNITCH, untwists the lid of the jar

full of ants, and then dumps the ants down THE SNITCH'S throat.

GERALD walks up to THE SNITCH with duck-tape and tapes his mouth completely shut. THE SNITCH can feel the fire-ants crawling and biting inside of him but he cannot move at all because of the unique paralysis-agent flowing through his system...

                    THE SNITCH
                 (yelling through
                  the duck-tape)
          Mmm!!! Mmm!!!

GERALD and VITO take off their black latex-gloves and spark their joints...BRODY sparks his COHIBA; they start smoking again. They just stand and watch THE SNITCH.

                                        CUT TO:

Fire-ants start crawling out from under THE SNITCH'S eye-lid...

                                        CUT TO:

INT. BRODY'S BAR - NIGHT

BRODY is sitting in a big booth in the back of a BAR, while GERALD and VITO are standing guard for him to the side the booth. It is BRODY'S BAR. It is a nice laid-back joint. MICKEY approaches GERALD, VITO, and BRODY at the booth. GERALD and VITO let MICKEY by. MICKEY sits down. He has BRODY'S BRIEFCASE...

                    MICKEY
                  (sincerely)
          How's it going, BRODY?

                    BRODY
                (with authority)
          You got my shit?

                    MICKEY
          Yeah, the job was fun, it was for
          kicks.

                    BRODY
          Good. Let me see the case.

                                        CUT TO:

INT. BRODY'S BAR - CONTINUOUS

MICKEY places the BRIEFCASE on the table and slides it to
BRODY. BRODY grabs the BRIEFCASE, unlocks it and opens it.

                                        CUT TO:

                    BRODY
          Attaboy. Looks like we're in
          business, MICKEY.

BRODY looks at the contents of the case in awe. There is
light shining from the BRIEFCASE onto BRODY'S face and in
his eyes. The contents of the case are unknown to MICKEY.
GERALD and VITO stand quietly with their backs turned.

                    BRODY
              (very satisfied)
          This is more like it.

BRODY closes the BRIEFCASE.

                                        CUT TO:

INT. BRODY'S BAR - CONTINUOUS

BRODY and MICKEY talk business.

                    BRODY
          Where's the money?

                    MICKEY
          It's safe and sound.

                    BRODY
          Good. You boys get to keep the
          cash-loot, and I keep the
          BRIEFCASE, as agreed.

                    MICKEY
          Not a problem. Thanks for the job,
          BRODY. You got any other jobs
          coming up for us?

                    BRODY
          As a matter of fact, I do. I got
          one coming up and I think you'll
          be perfect for the job.

                    MICKEY
          What kind of job we talking about?

                    BRODY
I got a bank-job; it's extremely
high-value.

                    MICKEY
            (arrogantly)
Come on, BRODY, you know we're the
best at what we do. I'll do the
job for shits and giggles. What's
the area?

                    BRODY
Sunset and 4th.

                    MICKEY
What's the score?

                    BRODY
Nice. Real nice, my boy.

                    MICKEY
What's the guard count?

                    BRODY
Six guards.

                    MICKEY
            (looking confused)
Damn, that's pretty loaded for a
bank-job.

                    BRODY
Well, my friend, this is not a
simple grab-and-go bank-job.

                    MICKEY
What are we talking about?

                    BRODY
            (quietly)
Twenty-five million in gold-bars.

                    MICKEY
            (eyes opened wide)
Holy shit, are you fucking with
me, BRODY?

                    BRODY
Do I look like I'm fucking with
you? I'm as serious as can be...25
million. Think of what you can do
with a percentage of that.

                    MICKEY
What will be our percentage?

                    BRODY
10%, no more-no less. That's 2.5
million for you three.

                    MICKEY
Now, that's what I like to here.
You know, BRODY, I think after
this job, with a cut like that, I
may finally be able to retire for
good. What do you think?

                    BRODY
          (lights a COHIBA)
It's your life, kid. We've been
doing business for years, I took
you under my wing. I've helped you
out, you've helped me out. I want
nothing more than to see you
happy, and prosperous. You are
like a son to me. If you want to
retire after this job, go ahead...
          (puffing his
          COHIBA)
...But, remember that there better
not be any fuck ups on the job;
not one fuck up. This one has to
be as clean as a nun on a
missionary-trip.

                    MICKEY
I understand, BRODY. We'll take
the job.

                    BRODY
Don't you need to consult DRE and
CARTER first?

                    MICKEY
          (arrogantly)
No. Those guys we'll be just fine.
With a cut like that, they won't
be able to resist. Plus they would
follow me into a burning building
if I asked them to, so we're
straight.

                    BRODY
Good. Now, I'm going to need you
guys to prepare for this job
quickly. It'll take place exactly
two days from now. I already got a
                    (MORE)

                    BRODY (cont'd)
driver ready. Whatever you need,
I'll provide, kid. Just do the
job, and do it right...

                    MICKEY
I got you, BRODY.

                    BRODY
Good. Now, you boys get your shit
together and get my gold.

                    MICKEY
Not a problem.

                    BRODY
And, MICKEY, if you boys fuck up
in any way, then I will retire you
myself.

                    MICKEY
Understood.

MICKEY stands up from the BAR-booth and walks toward the
exit. He exits BRODY'S BAR.

                              CUT TO:

EXT. CITY STREET - MOMENTS LATER

MICKEY is walking down a CITY STREET.

A MAN, HOMIE #1, intentionally bumps into MICKEY...

The MAN is with several other HOMIES.

The HOMIES are gang-bangers: BLOODS.

                    HOMIE #1
What the fuck, man?
          (pulls a blade)
Watch where you're going,
lil-nigga...

                    MICKEY
          (condescending)
Kid, watch your mouth. And put
that knife down before you hurt
yourself.

                    HOMIE #1
          Kid???
                (laughs)
          Yo, let's squash this nigga.

The HOMIE #1 and the 6 other HOMIES surround MICKEY...

                    MICKEY
                (smirking)
          You guys wanna die tonight?

The street is on the outskirts of town. However, there are
some people around, but, they just keep on walking by,
minding their own business.

                    HOMIE #1
                (directs the
                 others)
          Get em...

                                        CUT TO:

HOMIE#3 attacks MICKEY.

MICKEY immediately pulls a blade, and stabs HOMIE#3 directly
in the heart. HOMIE#3 dies on-the-spot.

MICKEY takes the blade and throws it at HOMIE#7, hitting him
square in the left eye-ball, killing him instantly.

MICKEY then runs up to the leader, HOMIE#1, and picks him up
by the neck. He breaks his neck with ease. MICKEY does this
all in a matter of seconds.

                                        CUT TO:

HOMIES#2,4,5,and 6 start to pull guns...

Before they can, MICKEY pulls his pistol, Eastwood-style,
and shoots all 4 men in the blink of an eye.

All 4 collapse, almost in harmony.

                                        CUT TO:

MICKEY puts his gun back in the holster.

He walks up to HOMIE#7, and pulls the blade out his eye-ball
and puts the blade back in its sheath.

MICKEY then proceeds to simply walk off from the CHAOS that
just unfolded.

CUT TO:

EXT. CITY STREET - MOMENTS LATER

MICKEY is walking hastily...

He pulls out his cell-phone and calls BRODY. MICKEY knows BRODY will fix the situation.

BRODY answers after one ring...

                    BRODY
               (through the phone)
          Yes?

                    MICKEY
          Hey, BRODY. It is MICKEY. I gotta
          stop by. We gotta problem.

                    BRODY
          Come by my OFFICE, now, please.

                    MICKEY
          All right, I'll be there shortly.

BRODY hangs up...

                                        CUT TO:

INT. BRODY'S OFFICE - LATER

BRODY'S OFFICE is in his HOUSE.

MICKEY is somewhat frantic and he is pacing back-and-forth in BRODY'S OFFICE. BRODY is sitting calmly at his desk. The OFFICE door is shut.

                    MICKEY
          Listen, BRODY! I killed 7 guys!
          This is a major problem!
               (stressed and
                anxious)
          They tried to jump me. I had to
          act, or they would've killed me.

                    BRODY
               (smiling)
          Ah, so what. You killed some
          gang-bangers. No big deal. I'll
          clean it up, ASAP. You have
          nothing to worry about, son.

MICKEY looks at BRODY with a mean stare...

                    MICKEY
          How'd you know they were bangers?

                    BRODY
          Ah, just a wild-guess, kid.

                    MICKEY
          Oh, yeah?

The tension is brewing between MICKEY and BRODY...

                    BRODY
          Yeah.

MICKEY shakes his head in frustration. He knows something
isn't right.

                    MICKEY
          Can I have a drink?

                    BRODY
          Does a Polar-Bear shit in the
          snow?

                    MICKEY
          I reckon so, BRODY. I reckon so.

                    BRODY
          Fix it yourself.

                                        CUT TO:

MICKEY pours himself a drink: Whiskey...

He fills the glass to the brim, no ice...

                    BRODY
          Word to the wise, my young
          friend...to go against Me is to go
          against God.

                    MICKEY
          What are you getting at, BRODY?

                    BRODY
          Do you believe in Fear, MICKEY?

                    MICKEY
          No. No, I do not. I only believe
          in FREEDOM.

                         BRODY
                    (lights a COHIBA)
          --FREEDOM is an illusion.
          PETRONIUS once said: "It is Fear
          that first brought the gods into
          this world."
                    (smiles and puffs
                     his cigar)
          Even the gods fear me. So shall
          you, MICKEY. I AM FEAR.

                         MICKEY
          --Fear has the largest eyes.--

                         BRODY
                    (puffing his
                     COHIBA)
          --Yes, MICKEY. I see all. I hear
          all. I know all.

BRODY, with a hand-gesture, shoos MICKEY...

                         BRODY
                    (shooing MICKEY)
          You may leave now.

MICKEY chugs his drink, and slams the glass on the
table...the glass cracks...

                         MICKEY
                    (patronizing)
          You got it, boss.

MICKEY opens the door and starts to walk out of BRODY'S
OFFICE.

                         BRODY
          Hey, MICKEY.

                         MICKEY
                    (turns around and
                     faces BRODY)
          Yeah?

                         BRODY
                    (smiling)
          Good luck.

MICKEY doesn't respond. He turns around, walks out of the
OFFICE and exits BRODY'S HOUSE with a cold silence...

                                        CUT TO:

INT. DETECTIVE'S OFFICE - NIGHT

A DETECTIVE sits at his desk in his OFFICE thumping a
pencil. An OFFICER brings him a report.

                    DETECTIVE FRANKO
          What's this?

                    OFFICER
          There was a robbery at a BANK
          earlier, DETECTIVE FRANKO. You've
          been assigned to the case by the
          CHIEF.

                    DETECTIVE FRANKO
          Son of a bitch. Why do I get this
          one?

                    OFFICER
          That's between you and CHIEF
          BARNES.

The OFFICER leaves the DETECTIVE'S OFFICE. DETECTIVE FRANKO
skims over the report. Sees the surveillance-photos of the
masked robbers.

                    DETECTIVE FRANKO
                (talking to
                 himself)
          PRESIDENTIAL MASKS, huh? These
          guys must be the real deal.

The CHIEF spontaneously enters DETECTIVE FRANKO'S OFFICE.

                    DETECTIVE FRANKO
          How can I help you, CHIEF?

                    CHIEF BARNES
          You got what I sent you?

                    DETECTIVE FRANKO
          Yeah, these guys are good. The
          PRESIDENTIAL MASKS, that's
          classic.

                    CHIEF BARNES
          Tell me about it. So you going to
          go investigate the case, or what?

                    DETECTIVE FRANKO
          Come on, CHIEF, I'm useless for
          these sorts of cases. Why are you
          giving it to me?

                    CHIEF BARNES
        Well, you're our veteran-DETECTIVE
        so we need you to do your job like
        a veteran-DETECTIVE. Truth be told
        these guys are professionals, I
        know you're not going to catch
        them. I'm just going through the
        motions, and I expect you to do
        the same.

                    DETECTIVE FRANKO
        I understand, CHIEF. But, you know
        my retirement is in two weeks, so
        I'm just trying to lay-low.

                    CHIEF BARNES
        Well, I guess you've got a long
        two weeks ahead of you, huh?

                    DETECTIVE FRANKO
        I guess so, sir...

                    CHIEF BARNES
        I need you to go downstairs and
        talk to the witnesses. Then I need
        you to go to the crime-scene
        tomorrow morning. And, FRANKO, at
        least act like a cop. You never
        know, you might get some leads. If
        you do, you report to me.

                    DETECTIVE FRANKO
        OK, CHIEF. What about the FBI?

                    CHIEF BARNES
        What did I say, FRANKO? You report
        to me, the FBI can go fuck
        themselves, this is my town.

                    DETECTIVE FRANKO
        Yes, sir. If I find out anything,
        then I'll report directly to you.

                    CHIEF BARNES
        Good.

CHIEF BARNES leaves FRANKO'S OFFICE. FRANKO puts on his
coat, picks up the report and the surveillance-photos, grabs
his gun and then leaves his OFFICE.

                              CUT TO:

INT. POLICE-STATION - MOMENTS LATER

DETECTIVE FRANKO walks down the hall of the POLICE-STATION
to the INTERROGATION ROOM.

                                        CUT TO:

INT. INTERROGATION ROOM - MOMENTS LATER

FRANKO is sitting at a table in the INTERROGATION ROOM. He
is interviewing witnesses. He calls in a witness.

                    DETECTIVE FRANKO
               Claudia Sanchez, enter.

The witness enters.

                    DETECTIVE FRANKO
               OK, Miss Sanchez. So, you're a
               BANK TELLER and you were a direct
               witness to the crime, correct?

                    BANK TELLER
                 (stressed and
                  frightened)
               Y-y-yes, sir.

                    DETECTIVE FRANKO
               I'm DETECTIVE FRANKO. Miss
               Sanchez, can you tell me anything
               that might help me out? Can you
               tell me anything you may have
               heard or saw while the crime was
               taking place? Faces, tattoos,
               names, voices, or anything?

                    BANK TELLER
               There were three of them. They
               were wearing these
               MASKS...l-l-looking like the
               presidents: OBAMA, GEORGE BUSH,
               and BILL CLINTON.

The woman starts crying.

                    BANK TELLER
               The man...The man wearing the
               OBAMA MASK, he said something
               about "THE ELITE"; I think that's
               what they call themselves. The man
               wearing the OBAMA MASK was really
               scary. The others were scary,
               too. They were really
                         (MORE)

                    BANK TELLER (cont'd)
intimidating. They kept referring
to each other as "Mr. President",
"Mr. Bush", and "Mr. Clinton". I
didn't see any tattoos or anything
like that, because they were
wearing suits and gloves and those
creepy MASKS. They pointed their
guns at everybody and they were
yelling and shooting at the
ceiling. They were toying with us.
We had no choice but to open the
SAFE.

                    DETECTIVE FRANKO
The Elite? Is there anything else
you can tell me regarding the
perpatrators?

                    BANK TELLER
No, sir. All I can really say is
that they took all the cash, and
they took the BRIEFCASE that was
in the SAFE.

                    DETECTIVE FRANKO
BRIEFCASE? What was in this
BRIEFCASE?

                    BANK TELLER
I don't know, sir.

                    DETECTIVE FRANKO
Well, I thank you for your time,
Miss Sanchez. We will try to bring
these guys to justice. You may
leave now.

                    BANK TELLER
OK. I'm sorry I do not have more
information--it's just that I'm
still scared to death by what
happened.

                    DETECTIVE FRANKO
Don't you worry about it, Miss
Sanchez, you've been of great
help. I will do my best to find
these guys and I'm sorry they put
you in harm's way.

                    BANK TELLER
Thank you, DETECTIVE FRANKO.

                    DETECTIVE FRANKO
     No problem, Ma'am.

                    DETECTIVE FRANKO
                    (looking at the
                    surveillance-photos)
     Who the hell are these guys?

DETECTIVE FRANKO calls in the next witness.

                    DETECTIVE FRANKO
     Mr. Edwards, please enter...

                                        CUT TO:

INT. DETECTIVE FRANKO'S VEHICLE - MORNING

FRANKO pulls up to the BANK, parks and exits his VEHICLE...

                                        CUT TO:

EXT. BANK - MOMENTS LATER

FRANKO walks up the BANK-stairs, analyzing the exterior. He
crosses the yellow-tape and enters the BANK.

                                        CUT TO:

INT. BANK - MOMENTS LATER

Inside the BANK there are cops and FORENSIC SPECIALISTS all
around, along with more yellow-tape.

FRANKO walks around, and examines the crime-scene. He walks
to the SAFE. He enters the SAFE.

                                        CUT TO:

INT. SAFE - MOMENTS LATER

There is a forensic team in the SAFE. FRANKO and the team
discuss the scene.

                    DETECTIVE FRANKO
     What do we got, guys?

                    FORENSIC SPECIALIST 1
                    (condescending)
Well, obviously we have a robbery,
DETECTIVE.

                    DETECTIVE FRANKO
                    (raises
                     voice/being
                     facetious)
Everybody in the building beware,
we have a genius over here.
                    (switches to
                     serious)
You know what I mean, jackass. Do
you have any traces of who these
guys may be?

                    FORENSIC SPECIALIST 1
No. But, there have been several
banks done in this area exactly
like this one, perhaps, by the
same group of guys. The
surveillance-footage shows that
they used an AMBULANCE as their
getaway-vehicle. These guys are
good.

                    DETECTIVE FRANKO
I saw the surveillance-photos.
What do you think about the MASKS
these guys wear? Some
'Point-Break' type-shit, huh? From
what I've heard, The President,
and the two assholes that came
before him, robbed this bank.
Quite laughable, I'd say.

                    FORENSIC SPECIALIST 2
They're trying to send a message
to us. It's a symbolic robbery;
they're being theatrical. You need
to examine the
surveillance-footage, FRANKO. The
photos are nothing.

                    DETECTIVE FRANKO
What kind of message? And, I'll
check out the footage before I
leave.

                    FORENSIC SPECIALIST 2
Hard to say. The MASKS are the
least of our concerns, we're more
concerned with who's behind the
                    (MORE)

                    FORENSIC SPECIALIST 2 (cont'd)
          MASKS, as you should be,
          DETECTIVE.

                    FORENSIC SPECIALIST 3
          I believe they wear the MASKS
          because they're trying to be "the
          untouchable gang" dressed as
          presidents, that's my guess. They
          simply want to be remembered.
          Honestly, I don't think it was an
          independent job, I think they were
          hired.

                    DETECTIVE FRANKO
          Hired? Hired by who?

                    FORENSIC SPECIALIST 3
          I don't know, FRANKO, that's your
          job. Whoever it is, they know what
          they're doing.

                    DETECTIVE FRANKO
          Yep...

DETECTIVE FRANKO walks out of the SAFE, and further examines
the crime-scene.

                                        CUT TO:

INT. BANK SECURITY-ROOM - MOMENTS LATER

FRANKO is in the SECURITY-ROOM of the BANK. He is studying
the surveillance-footage. He is studying 'THE ELITE'.

DETECTIVE FRANKO sees they use an AMBULANCE, they're quick,
and they move with precision.

FRANKO is stunned by the footage. He stops the footage right
as MICKEY is looking into the camera with his dark eyes.
FRANKO observes MICKEY, and his OBAMA-MASK. The DETECTIVE is
deeply disturbed.

                    DETECTIVE FRANKO
                (ominous soliloquy)
          The Thief cometh not but to steal,
          kill, and to destroy.

                                        CUT TO:

INT. BANK - MOMENTS LATER

FRANKO takes out some black latex-gloves from his
coat-pocket and puts them on. He picks up a bullet shell and
examines it. He puts it back down. Right near the bullet
shell he discovers a random single piece of dark hair on the
floor of the BANK...

                  DETECTIVE FRANKO
    Bingo.

                            CUT TO:

FRANKO pulls out a small plastic-baggy and stealthily puts
the piece of hair in it. He quickly slips the plastic-baggy,
containing the hair, into his coat-pocket...

FRANKO removes his gloves and throws them in a waste-basket.

                  DETECTIVE FRANKO
    Well, my work is done here, boys.

                 FORENSIC SPECIALIST 1
          (talking under his
           breath)
    Lazy Bastard...

FRANKO walks toward the exit of the BANK.

                  DETECTIVE FRANKO
    I heard that, asshole!

FRANKO exits the BANK.

                            CUT TO:

EXT. BANK - MOMENTS LATER

FRANKO makes a call on his cell-phone to a FORENSIC EXAMINER
at the POLICE STATION.

                 FORENSIC EXAMINER
          (through the phone)
    Hello?

                  DETECTIVE FRANKO
          (into the phone)
    Hey, it's FRANKO. Do you think you
    can do something for me? I need a
    piece of hair analyzed...

                    FORENSIC EXAMINER
                  (through the phone)
          Yeah, FRANKO, bring it on by, I'll
          see what I can do.

                    DETECTIVE FRANKO
                  (into the phone)
          All right, I'll be there in 20.

FRANKO enters his VEHICLE and takes off from the
yellow-taped BANK...

                                        CUT TO:

INT. POLICE-STATION LABORATORY - LATER

FRANKO waits patiently for the results of the DNA test.

                    FORENSIC EXAMINER
          We have a match, sir.

                    DETECTIVE FRANKO
          Who is it?

                    FORENSIC EXAMINER
          A MICKEY MONTANA.

                    DETECTIVE FRANKO
          MICKEY MONTANA? Never heard of
          him. Print me off a copy of his
          rap-sheet, I want to take a closer
          look at it.

                    FORENSIC EXAMINER
          All right.

The FORENSIC EXAMINER prints off a copy of MICKEY'S
rap-sheet and hands it to FRANKO.

                    DETECTIVE FRANKO
          Thanks for your help.

                    FORENSIC EXAMINER
          Not a problem.

DETECTIVE FRANKO exits the POLICE-STATION LABORATORY and
heads upstairs to his OFFICE to examine MICKEY'S rap-sheet.

                                        FADE TO BLACK:

                                        CHAPTER TITLE
                                        APPEARANCE:

III. THE GRIM REEFER

                                        FADE IN:

INT. 2012 YELLOW CHEVY CAMARO - DAY

GERALD and VITO are cruising down a city street in the 2012
YELLOW CHEVY CAMARO. GERALD is driving.

                    VITO
              (in mid-discussion)
          -So, now that it has passed in
          those states, people can smoke
          reefer legally? Recreationally?

                    GERALD
          Yeah, basically. Colorado and
          Washington State passed some shit
          that legalized it recreationally.
          Hell, it's bout legal in half the
          country on a medical level.
          Eventually, we'll be able to buy
          marijuana-cigarettes at the
          grocery store. Soon it'll be
          legalized, for recreational
          purposes, in all 50 states; no
          doubt in my mind. Marijuana
          prohibition hasn't worked, and
          nationwide legalization of pot is
          inevitable. I give it 12 years,
          and the whole damn nation will be
          free to smoke weed in peace.

                    VITO
              (curious)
          Hell, yeah, man. How about
          purchasing it? How is that gonna
          work when it's fully legalized
          nationwide? Will we be able to
          just walk into a convenient store
          and pick up as much green as we
          want?

                    GERALD
          Nah, it's not like that. It'll be
          treated more like alcohol, but
          more strict. Essentially, if
          you're 21 or over and have a valid
          ID, you'd be eligible to go into a
          marijuana dispensary and purchase
          up to an ounce of reefer; the laws
          limit the amount people can
          purchase. And, the growers are
                    (MORE)

                    GERALD (cont'd)
only allowed to grow so much
within a certain amount of square
footage. But, other than that,
it's pretty lax. And, as time
passes the laws will become even
more lax.

                    VITO
Hell, yeah, brother.

                    GERALD
Hell, yeah. I'm just ready for it
to be legal nationwide. This
country, this motherfucking World
needs legal marijuana.

                    VITO
That's the American-Dream: Work
hard, get cash, sit back, relax,
and smoke mary-jane.

                    GERALD
Legal or illegal, America is still
the land of the free, and the home
of the high...America is a
business, and marijuana will soon
be its greatest commodity, besides
Pussy. This country should be
called 'The United States of
AMERIJUANA'. Marijuana will rule
this century, the next century,
and beyond; mark my words.

                    VITO
Damn, GERALD, that's some deep
shit you just said. Hell, I agree
with you completely. And, it's
stupid that the government has
demonized marijuana for so long,
and it has taken damn-near 80
years for legalization to happen
in the states it has happened in.
But, it's still awesome to see
legalization of pot in my
lifetime, and to know the movement
is progressing. You're right,
GERALD, marijuana is going to rule
the world; I think forever.

                    GERALD
Yep. And, it's not just the
government that is against it.
Primarily, it is the Timber
                    (MORE)

                    GERALD (cont'd)
industry, the Tobacco industry,
and the Drug Cartels that are
holding nationwide marijuana
legalization back. The Timber
Industry wants to prevent the boom
of Hemp. The Tobacco Industry
wants to prevent the boom of legal
marijuana-cigarettes. And, The
Cartels want to stop marijuana
from becoming a legal drug in The
States, because they'll lose
massive profits...

                    VITO
              (reaching into his
               coat pocket)
Yeah, man, that's the truth. But,
speaking of which, I got something
right here...
              (pulls out a fat
               joint)
...Let's light it up before we do
the job.

VITO lights the joint.

                    GERALD
              (wanting to smoke)
Hell, yeah.

VITO tokes the joint a few times to get it lit, and then
passes it to GERALD...

                    VITO
              (passes the joint
               to GERALD)
This'll fix our altitude.

                    GERALD
Cool, my nigga.
              (hits the joint
               twice and passes
               it to VITO)
Damn, that's a taste of Heaven.

                    VITO
              (puffs the joint
               twice and then
               passes it to
               GERALD)
It is some Lemon Kush. Very, very
good shit.

                              GERALD
                         (puffs the joint
                          twice and passes
                          it)
               Damn, Lemon.
                         (exhales and
                          coughs)
               Umm Umm...Good shit, my brother.

                              VITO
               Hell, man, I might be too high to
               do this job, now.

                              GERALD
                         (hits the joint
                          two more times)
               Stop tripping, man, it's your
               joint. Lemon Kush, in most cases,
               has a perfect equilibrium of CBD
               and THC. So, even being high, you
               should be able to function maybe
               even better than when you ain't
               high.
                         (puts the joint
                          out)
               I'm gonna put it out for now, and
               we'll smoke the rest after the job
               is done.

                              VITO
               All right, brother. Hey, what the
               fuck is CBD?

VITO is really high, as is GERALD. They're as high as the
Himalayas...

                              GERALD
               Cannibidiol. It's the secondary
               ingredient to THC...

                              VITO
               You're a marijuana encyclopedia,
               my friend.

                              GERALD
               No, my brother, I'm a marijuana
               connoisseur.

VITO rubs his hands on his face as if he is sleepy; he's
just really stoned.

                    VITO
              (changes topic)
     I can't believe that BRODY is
     giving those assholes that job. I
     mean, have we not proven that we
     are the people for that kind of
     work? BRODY should just let us get
     it done.

                    GERALD
     Yeah, definitely. But truth is,
     man, I think we're too good and
     we're too lethal for that kind of
     job. BRODY doesn't want any
     liabilities or casualties you know
     what I'm saying? If we were to do
     the job, then we would end up
     doing damage. We're hitmen, not
     bank robbers.

                    VITO
     That's understandable, but I still
     don't trust those fuckers. There
     is something about them, I just
     can't pinpoint it. MICKEY has
     betrayal written all over his
     face. He's loyal, but I can sense
     that he also envies BRODY.

                    GERALD
     Hey, that's between you, BRODY and
     MICKEY. I know that BRODY knows
     what he is doing, though.

                    VITO
     Yeah, I guess you're right. BRODY
     is like a living, breathing
     crystal-ball. He's fucking
     omniscient. He's damn-near
     omnipotent. But, I just got this
     itch that MICKEY is trying to
     cross BRODY. I don't trust that
     guy as far as I can throw him. I
     think he is up to something.

                    GERALD
     Man, you worry too much.

                    VITO
              (pointing to his
               temple with his
               index finger)
     It's all instinct, my brother...

                    GERALD
Instinct, my ass, man. You're full
of shit.

                    VITO
            (very serious)
We'll see. Anyway, man, are we
close to the spot?

                    GERALD
Yeah, it's right up here on the
left.

                    VITO
So, what's the best bud you've
ever smoked?

                    GERALD
I copped some "Cat Piss" up in New
York once. Man, that shit had me
twisted...

                    VITO
I've heard of it--I actually read
of it in "High Times". The best
bud I've ever smoked was this shit
that my cousin MICHAEL grew. It
didn't even have a name. He
harvested about 20 pounds of it.
Dude is a mad scientist. The stuff
he grew had me high for two days
straight off one joint, no lie.
That was the best dope I've ever
smoked, hands-down. Everything he
grows is pure-dank.

                    GERALD
            (kind of shocked)
Damn! You need to hook me up with
ya boy!

                    VITO
Hell, I would man, but I haven't
even seen him in almost 20 years.
He went into the military back in
96', and, poof, he disappeared;
none of the family has seen or
talked to him since. I'm sure I'll
see MICHAEL again eventually, so,
hell, maybe one day I'll be able
to get you the hook up.

                         GERALD
               Cool, brother. Well, let's get
               ready.

The two MEN pull up to an APARTMENT COMPLEX. GERALD drives
around the APARTMENT COMPLEX parking-lot and he parks the
2012 YELLOW CHEVY CAMARO. He and VITO then exit the VEHICLE.

                                        CUT TO:

EXT. APARTMENT COMPLEX - MOMENTS LATER

This APARTMENT COMPLEX is in the projects of LA...

The place is gritty and very rough; filled with nothing but
killers and dealers...

VITO and GERALD proceed to walk up the STAIRWELL of the
APARTMENT COMPLEX.

                                        CUT TO:

INT. STAIRWELL - CONTINUOUS

GERALD is walking up the STAIRWELL quite fast and VITO
struggles to keep up...

                         VITO
               So what APARMENT is it?

                         GERALD
               616.

                         VITO
               Damn, and there's no elevator is
               there?

                         GERALD
               No. You'll be all right, man, it's
               just 6 floors. Quit complaining,
               and get your game-face on.

                         VITO
               All right, my fault, man...I'm
               just high. And, I'm drained from
               last night.--

                         GERALD
               --Drained from what, nigga?

                    VITO
Man, Alicia came over last night.
We got pretty fucked up and hopped
off the good foot and did the bad
thing. She had me up all night.

                    GERALD
And you're complaining about that?

                    VITO
Come on, man, you know how it is.
Your girl comes over, you drink
some Crown, bump some coke, next
thing you know you're fucking six
ways from Sunday.

                    GERALD
           (very serious)
You know that I'm married,
motherfucker.

                    VITO
Oh, yeah, my bad. How is your wife
anyway?

                    GERALD
She's good, but let's discuss that
later. We're here to handle
business.

                    VITO
I got you, man, I'm slipping.

                    GERALD
Yeah. Get your shit straight, man.

                    VITO
           (out of breath)
All right, brother, my fault I'm
just high as shit. What are we on?
The 4th floor?

                    GERALD
Yeah, I told you it wasn't so bad,
only two more floors to go. I know
you're high as shit, man. Your
damn eyes are red as the devil's
dick. You need some Visine, nigga.

                    VITO
Are you asking me that, or telling
me?

                    GERALD
          I'm telling you, motherfucker.
          Now, get your shit together.

                    VITO
          So, you don't have any?

                    GERALD
          No, I don't have any motherfucking
          eye-drops! You're a hitman,
          you're not about to go into a job
          that requires you to not look
          high, man.

                    VITO
          All right, I'm good, chill, chill,
          brother. I just feel as if I'm
          fading away...

                    GERALD
                (getting pissed)
          Man, Goddamn. I'm pretty high
          myself, and you don't hear me
          crying like a little-bitch. Pull
          yourself together.

                    VITO
                (takes a deep
                 breath)
          Okay.
                (exhales)
          Okay, I got this.

VITO and GERALD are nearing their destination: APARTMENT 616

                    GERALD
                (curious and
                 extremely high)
          Nigga, where did you get that bud,
          anyway?

                    VITO
          I got it from my guy outta
          COMPTON.

                    GERALD
          That's some strong reefer. But,
          enough talking, let's get ready,
          for real, man.

GERALD and VITO walk up the last two sets of stairs and go
down the HALLWAY toward APARTMENT 616.

                                        CUT TO:

INT. HALLWAY - MOMENTS LATER

GERALD and VITO are moving casually down the HALLWAY...

                    VITO
          One last thing, GERALD.

                    GERALD
          After the job, VITO.

                    VITO
          All right.

The HITMEN arrive at APARTMENT 616. VITO stands behind
GERALD. GERALD knocks at the door.

                    VITO
          Shit...

                    GERALD
          Damn, man, now what is it?

                    VITO
          I need some water...

                    GERALD
          Damn, you're a needy
          motherfucker...

A MAN opens the door. GERALD and VITO invite themselves into
the APARTMENT; they just walk right in...

                                        CUT TO:

INT. APARTMENT 616 - MOMENTS LATER

GERALD and VITO intimidatingly enter APARTMENT ROOM 616.

The MAN shuts the door behind them.

The place is quite small and doesn't have much space.

                    GERALD
               (assertive)
          Hello, gentlemen. Are we
          interrupting?

There are four young MEN in the APARTMENT. They are black.
Two are sitting on a sofa, one has opened the door, and the

other is in the kitchen-area. Their names are CHAD, TREY, JOHN, and TRAVIS. A television is on: "Tom and Jerry" is playing.

                                        CUT TO:

                    TRAVIS
                (confused)
        Who the hell are you?

                    GERALD
                (with authority)
        I'm The Devil. This is my
        partner...
                (points thumb at
                VITO)
        ...The Grim Reaper. We've come to
        collect your souls for BRODY. Do
        you know BRODY?

                    CHAD
                (talking to GERALD
                and VITO)
        Oh, shit, man. Listen we apologize
        for any fuck ups that happened
        between us and BRODY. We didn't
        intend to mess up the deal. We got
        caught up in something, and we had
        to do what we had to do. No hard
        feelings. It's just business.
        Whatever we owe BRODY, we'll pay
        it back ten-fold.

                    GERALD
        What's your name, lil nigga?

                    CHAD
        CHAD.

                    GERALD
        Oh, so you must be the spokesmen
        for the group. The negotiator. The
        leader, if you will. I have a
        question for you CHAD: Do I look
        like a businessman?

                                        CUT TO:

The four MEN look at GERALD with fear written all over their faces.

                    CHAD
          No, sir, you do not look like a
          businessman.

                    GERALD
          Good answer, because the truth is,
          kid, I'm not a businessman. But,
          do you know who is?

                    CHAD
          Who's that, sir?

GERALD pulls a 9mm glock and starts pacing back and forth.
VITO stands to the side patiently and quietly with his hands
down and crossed.

                    GERALD
          My 9mm glock is a businessman. It
          means business. Beautiful, ain't
          it. You know, I remember the first
          time I killed a man. It was
          actually with this weapon, here.
          It's been a long time since then,
          but I still remember that feeling
          of taking that man's life. It's
          odd to say this, but I believe I
          literally saw his soul ascend from
          his body. It was amazing. I never
          thought I could kill a man, but
          once I did I felt pretty damn
          good. You ever had that feeling,
          CHAD?

CHAD hesitates to respond.

                    CHAD
               (in great fear)
          N-n-no, sir...

                    GERALD
               (with great
                conviction)
          Any of you boys ever read 'The
          Four Loves'?

                                        CUT TO:

The four MEN look at each other in confusion. GERALD doesn't
give them time to respond.

                    GERALD
          Of course you haven't. You kids
          are too busy "tweeting" nowadays.
          Anyway, according to C.S Lewis,
                    (MORE)

                    GERALD (cont'd)
the author, there are four loves:
Charity, Affection, Eros, and
Friendship.

                    VITO
Preach it, brother. Oh, you kids
mind if I smoke in here?

                    TREY
              (dazed and
               confused)
Uh...

                    VITO
              (lights his
               cigarette)
I take that as a yes.

                    GERALD
              (looking VITO)
All right, VITO, be quiet, man,
I'm trying to drop some wisdom on
these kids.

                    VITO
              (opens hand to
               GERALD to carry
               on)
My fault, brother, continue.

                                   CUT TO:

GERALD is still pacing.

                    GERALD
              (looks each of the
               four MEN
               eye-to-eye)
As I was saying. There are four
loves. Each of these loves came
from God. According to the author,
we love because we need to love.
Also, C.S Lewis goes on to point
out that: as we are created in
God's image, we as human beings
need to be loved. You following
me, brother-man?

The four MEN are now a nervous-wreck.

                    GERALD
          Also, he intelligently points out
          that the reason we love is because
          God loves. We were made in God's
          image. God is love--and we love
          because God created us to love. Do
          you know why God created us?

                    JOHN
          I don't believe in God.

                    GERALD
          Oh really. Well, my friend, you
          should. Now, allow me to provide
          you an answer to my question. God
          created us out of the same basic
          desire we have as human beings; he
          needed to love, and he needed to
          be loved. Pretty simple, right?

                    CHAD
          I guess so. So what's your point?

                    GERALD
          Well, my friends, God is Love. He
          endowed us with the ability to
          love. But on the other hand he
          installed in us the ability to
          sin. In my strict opinion, the
          four loves are the counter-balance
          to the seven deadly sins. You do
          know the seven deadly sins, don't
          you?

The four MEN look blank. They look at each other in panic.
GERALD cocks his gun and points it at the two MEN sitting on
the couch.

                    VITO
               (smoking heavily)
          He asked you guys a question. It
          would be wise to answer.

                    TREY
          O-o-OK. The seven deadly sins are
          Gluttony, Lust, Pride, Greed,
          Wrath, Envy, and Sloth.

                    GERALD
          Way to go, brother-man. You think
          you're pretty smart, huh?

                    TREY
                (fearful)
No, man, just please tell us what
you want so you can--so you can
leave.

                    GERALD
                (serious as can be)
I'll leave when you boys are
deceased. As I said before,
friendo, I have come to collect
your souls. Did you think I was
kidding? Anyway, back to my point.
See, we're just human beings. We
love and we sin. We cannot stop
ourselves from loving, just as we
cannot stop ourselves from
sinning. But, sinning is one
thing; sinning against God is pure
blasphemy. Loving is one thing;
loving God is the path to
salvation. See, when you just
plain ole' sin, God forgives you
because he is love. But when you
sin against God, then until you
repent, you will not be granted
forgiveness. He loves you no
matter what. But sinning against
God is tantamount to committing
suicide, and he cannot forgive you
unless you repent.

                    CHAD
What are you getting at, sir?

                    GERALD
                (scratching his
                 head with his
                 pistol)
Well, it's simple, boys. You all
have sinned against God. In this
world, BRODY is God. You
intentionally fucked BRODY over,
which is equivalent to fucking God
over. Now, I don't know the
specifics, and I really don't care
to know the specifics. Like I said
before, I'm no businessman. I'm
not here to negotiate. I'm not
here to reconcile anything. I'm
here to punish all of you. See, no
matter how powerful BRODY may
seem, he is just as dependent upon
you as you are upon him. BRODY
                    (MORE)

                         GERALD (cont'd)
          loves you guys. He needs you, and
          he needs to be needed by you. But,
          as the sinful creatures that you
          are, you sinned against him and,
          for that, he cannot forgive you.
          The only way you can get out of
          your punishment is by committing
          suicide. But you technically
          already have because you have
          sinned against the God.

                                      CUT TO:

VITO smirks, takes one last hit from his cigarette and
throws it on the carpet and stomps it out...

                         GERALD
                    (with authority)
          Now, before you kids try anything
          stupid, remember that my glock is
          a businessman. My partner The Grim
          Reaper has also brought a
          businessman. This visit is nothing
          personal, it's strictly business.
          I'm sure you boys understand. You
          move, you're dead. You don't move,
          you're dead. This is a lose-lose
          situation. But remember you
          brought this upon yourselves when
          you sinned against the Almighty.

VITO pulls out his pistol and cocks it.

                         CHAD
                    (frantic)
          No! Please, sir, we will make it
          up to BRODY! Just tell him that we
          fucked up and we'll make things
          right!

                         GERALD
                    (with great
                     conviction)
          Your repentance is too late. Your
          punishment is now.

                                      CUT TO:

GERALD nods at VITO. The two HITMEN hold up their pistols
and proceed to shoot and kill the four young MEN...

                                      CUT TO:

EXT. APARTMENT 616 - MOMENTS LATER

GERALD and VITO exit the APARTMENT 616. They both check
their shoes for blood and wipe them on the door-mat.

                                        CUT TO:

INT. HALLWAY - CONTINUOUS

GERALD and VITO walk down the HALLWAY toward the STAIRWELL
of the APARTMENT COMPLEX.

                    VITO
            Fucking kids. I hate we had to do
            that. But, hey, you fuck with
            BRODY, you get fucked.

                    GERALD
            That's the way it goes, business
            is business.

                    VITO
            Yeah, true.

GERALD and VITO start walking down the STAIRWELL of the
APARTMENT COMPLEX.

                                        CUT TO:

INT. STAIRWELL - MOMENTS LATER

GERALD and VITO walk down the STAIRWELL, cool, calm and
collected.

                    VITO
            Hey, man, let's resume the
            conversation we were having.

                    GERALD
            What conversation?

                    VITO
            What I was telling you about
            Alicia before we got to the room.
            I wasn't finished.

                    GERALD
            Listen, man, you're my dear
            friend. But, I refuse to listen to
            you talk about your sexual
            escapades. Plus, I already know
            all there is to know about women;
                    (MORE)

                    GERALD (cont'd)
especially the ones you're
fucking...

                    VITO
               (laughing)
Man, how do you know all there is
to know about women, and the ones
I'm fucking?

                    GERALD
Ok. There are two types of women.
There are ladies who try to be
freaks. And there are freaks who
try to be ladies. Basically, you
have ladies who try to be naughty,
freaky, and nasty--then on the
other hand, you have freaks who
try to be lady-like. The freaks
who try to be ladies are the ones
you want. They're the lawyers,
nurses, school teachers, quiet
chicks, so-on-so forth. The ladies
who try to be freaks are the
fucked up chicks who do dope,
drink, and party like hell. They
don't know what they want in life,
so they fuck and suck guys
day-in-day-out trying to be a
freak, when in reality they are a
lady. The freaks who try to be
ladies, typically, are monogamous.
They look for one man at a time to
be freaky with all the time. They
have the conservative clothes,
good-manners, and such, but when
they get you in the bedroom, they
fuck your brains out. Freaks that
try to be ladies have the
intellect for Love. Ladies who try
to be freaks are lost-causes. You
know what I'm saying?

                    VITO
Damn, man, I never thought about
it like that. It's complex, but
simple at the same time. So, what
do you think about Alicia? Is she
a lady that's trying to be a
freak, or a freak that's trying to
be a lady?

                    GERALD
          Well, man, I don't know the girl
          like that. I've seen her only a
          couple times. Hell, I couldn't
          really tell you. But, considering
          what you were telling me earlier,
          she sounds like a lady that is
          trying to be a freak. Which is No
          Bueno, mi Amigo.

                    VITO
          Damn, I had a feeling you were
          going to say that.

                    GERALD
          Ah, shit, man. Don't sweat it. My
          philosophy about women isn't
          universal. Shit, you never know,
          you might end up putting a ring on
          her finger, or some shit. My words
          aren't absolute, do what you do,
          you know what I'm saying? That's
          your girl. You shouldn't let my
          advice affect what you got going
          on.

                    VITO
          I appreciate it, GERALD. You want
          to know something, man?

                    GERALD
          What's that?

                    VITO
          You're a good friend, man. Thank
          you for your friendship,
          brother.--

GERALD and VITO get to the last step and start walking
toward the 2012 YELLOW CHEVY CAMARO.

                                        CUT TO:

EXT. APARTMENT COMPLEX - CONTINUOUS

GERALD and VITO move calmly to their VEHICLE.

                    GERALD
          --No problem, my brother. Now quit
          being soft on me. Let's go meet up
          with BRODY and let him know the
          job is done.

                         VITO
          I'm not being soft, man, I'm just
          letting you know I appreciate your
          friendship. Anyway, like you said,
          let's go meet with the Boss-man.

GERALD and VITO get into the 2012 YELLOW CHEVY CAMARO and
they ride off from the APARTMENT COMPLEX.

                                        CUT TO:

EXT. THE DARK WOODS/DREAM SEQUENCE - NIGHT

It is snowing. The night sky is dark as the abyss. However,
there are many stars shining bright in the darkness. Also,
the Moon is full; it is a luminous blood-Moon.

MICKEY opens his eyes. He is lying on his back in the snow,
surrounded by tall trees. He is deep in the forest: THE DARK
WOODS. He sits up and looks around. He hears something
coming toward him from the shadows.

Suddenly, a Pale-Horse appears from out of the shadows of
THE DARK WOODS and walks toward MICKEY. It stops about 10
feet away from MICKEY. The Pale-Horse is absolutely
beautiful. Its eyes are made of fire. The Horse is whiter
than the snow that is falling. It is breathing and exhaling
smoke and fire.

MICKEY stands up and looks at The Pale-Horse in awe. He
notcies that there is a hooded-HORSEMAN, dressed in
all-black, sitting on The Pale-Horse...

THE HORSEMAN'S eyes are blood-red and glowing, yet MICKEY
cannot see his face...

                         MICKEY
                       (perplexed)
                    Who are You?

THE HORSEMAN lifts his hood and reveals himself. He is the
mirror-image of MICKEY except his eyes are red. THE HORSEMAN
blinks once and his eyes turn solid-black.

                       THE HORSEMAN
          I AM WHO I AM.

As soon as THE HORSEMAN utters those words the snow
spontaneously transforms into fire and the trees get
scorched. Yet, MICKEY is untouched by the flames. The fire
surrounds MICKEY, THE HORSEMAN, and The Pale-Horse.

                         MICKEY
                      (in awe)
              What the Hell???

                      THE HORSEMAN
              He that dies pays all debts. He
              that becomes Death, defeats Death.
              BECOME DEATH.

The Pale-Horse neighs and turns THE HORSEMAN away from
MICKEY. The Pale-Horse takes THE HORSEMAN into the raging
fire.

The beastly animal and the ghostly rider disappear into the
flames.

As soon as THE HORSEMAN and The Pale-Horse vanish, the fire
engulfs MICKEY and he feels the full power of Hell-Fire.

                         MICKEY
                      (burning alive)
                 AaHHH!!!

                                            CUT TO:

INT. MICKEY'S HOUSE/DREAM SEQUENCE - MORNING

MICKEY shakes around in a cold-sweat.

He finally opens his eyes. He is astonished and dumbfounded
by what he saw in his dream, as it was extremely lucid.

                         MICKEY
                      (dumbfounded)
                 Damn, what a fucking dream...

Sunlight is penetrating his room all around. He lies on his
Master-Bed, and yawns...

He gets up and does his morning routine; sips coffee, smokes
a joint, so-on-so-forth.

MICKEY then hops in the shower.

                                            CUT TO:

INT. MICKEY'S HOUSE/DREAM SEQUENCE - MOMENTS LATER

MICKEY exits the shower. He wraps his towel around his
waist. He then stops, and looks into the mirror. It is
blurry from all the steam on it.

MICKEY wipes the moisture off the mirror very slowly. After he wipes the mirror several times, BRODY appears with a smirk on his face.

Seeing BRODY scares the Hell out of MICKEY...

MICKEY fears nothing. He only fears BRODY...

> MICKEY
> (shocked by
> BRODY'S
> appearance)
> AaHHH!!!!!!

Blood pours out of BRODY'S eyes...

> BRODY
> (with a demonic
> voice-tone)
> I got you now, you little-shit!

BRODY reaches through the mirror and shatters the glass of it, revealing darkness behind him.

BRODY grabs MICKEY and pulls him through the mirror into the darkness...

> CUT TO:

INT. MICKEY'S HOUSE - DAY

MICKEY snaps awake from his nap...

> MICKEY
> (startled)
> Holy Fuck!!!

> CUT TO:

INT. MICKEY'S HOUSE - LATER

MICKEY'S HOUSE is modest, and it is located in COMPTON.

MICKEY, despite being a robber, lives quite frugally.

CARTER and DRE are sitting on MICKEY'S couch. MICKEY pours himself, DRE, and CARTER glasses of SAILOR JERRY'S RUM. He has a bar in his HOUSE.

                    MICKEY
          Come get yourselves a drink,
          brothers.

DRE and CARTER get up from the couch to get their drinks and
then they sit back down on the couch.

MICKEY chugs his drink in a split-second and then pours
himself another.

                    MICKEY
          Okay, guys, this is how it'll go
          down: CARTER, you and I will
          handle the guards, and do crowd
          control. DRE, you'll handle the
          safe and collect the loot. CARTER
          if you get any dissent from any of
          the guards, knock their teeth down
          their throat. DRE, you be
          swift--and, remember that we are
          not after any cash--we are simply
          getting the gold-bars.

                    DRE
          I got you, MICKEY.

                    CARTER
          What about our driver?

                    MICKEY
          Don't worry about it, BRODY has us
          covered on that. The driver will
          pick us up at the safe-house which
          is about 5 miles from Sunset and
          4th. He'll drop us off and wait
          outside the BANK for us. We'll
          have to be quicker than usual,
          because this is a big job. After
          we get the gold, we'll go to our
          designated spot, and then we'll
          take out the driver as we always
          do.

MICKEY sips his drink.

                    MICKEY
          We have very little time to
          prepare for this job. This is the
          least time we've ever had, and I
          know it's a lot of pressure doing
          this thing so abruptly, but I know
          we can pull it off.

MICKEY gulps the rest of his drink, while CARTER and DRE begin sipping on theirs.

MICKEY pours himself another drink.

>   CARTER
>   Sounds good to me. Pressure makes
>   diamonds, as they say. What
>   disguises are we going with this
>   time around?

>   MICKEY
>   (arrogantly)
>   You guys know we have to rock the
>   PRESIDENTIAL MASKS. We're building
>   a legacy with those things.

>   CARTER
>   Hell-yeah. We've done three jobs
>   with those MASKS. We might as well
>   go out with a bang.

>   DRE
>   I'm still rocking the
>   CLINTON-MASK, as we all know Bill
>   Clinton is really black. Well,
>   mentally anyway.

MICKEY and CARTER bust out laughing at DRE.

>   CARTER
>   (laughing)
>   Of course he's black. Bill's a O.G
>   because he got head in the
>   oval-office and then had the
>   audacity to lie about it to The
>   World.

>   MICKEY
>   Yeah, I agree, Bill is a O.G.
>   Hell, I might as well run for
>   president. I don't think I could
>   do much worse or better than the
>   black-ass that's in there now.
>   Plus, I would love to get head in
>   the oval-office!

>   CARTER
>   Ain't that the truth. Speaking of
>   the oval-office, did you guys see
>   Mitt Romney got the Republican
>   nomination. Well, unofficially.
>   He's going to be running against
>   (MORE)

                    CARTER (cont'd)
Obama in November.

                    DRE
Man, fuck that guy and fuck Obama.

MICKEY downs the glass of RUM like it's water. He can drink
like a fish.

                    MICKEY
               (assertive)
Fuck em all. Fuck all the
presidents, man. Fuck the
Congress. Fuck the system.
               (passionate)
The Republicans and Democrats are
one. The World is ONE. All the
government leaders are all crooks,
especially the POTUS. Most all the
government leaders in this nation
and the world are corrupt. They
don't work for the people. They
work for those lawyers, bankers,
and gangsters, who pull the
strings behind the scenes. Fuck em
all, man. That's why we wear the
MASKS...to show how criminal the
presidents and the world leaders
really are; we show how phony the
system is. Obama will get
re-elected this year. In 2016
it'll be Hillary Clinton vs.
Donald Trump--

                    CARTER
--Donald Trump???

                    MICKEY
               (with conviction)
--Yep. And Donald Trump will win
the presidency in 2016. Trump,
Hillary and Obama are in league
with the bankers. It's all rigged.
It's all a charade. The presidents
are puppets, plain and simple. All
those in power are simply pawns in
a rigged chess-game. But, mark my
words: Donald Trump will be
elected president in 2016. And,
Obama will get re-elected this
November. By wearing the MASKS, we
show the true nature of the
presidency, power, and 'THE ELITE'
groups that control the world.
                    (MORE)

                    MICKEY (cont'd)
They're nothing but a bunch of
thieves, liars, killers, and
destroyers. They don't want us to
be free. In the eyes of those in
power: FREEDOM is SLAVERY. They
want us all to be slaves...

                    DRE
               (in disbelief)
Whatever you say, MICKEY.

                    MICKEY
Yep. Whatever I say.

CARTER and DRE gulp the rest of their drinks down.

                    MICKEY
I'm telling you, DRE. The
president, whoever it is, is just
a errand-boy for the bankers.
Those bankers know nothing but
control, corruption, and profits.
They don't care about you, me, or
anybody else. Those motherfuckers
want to take over the world. You
see what I'm getting at?

                    DRE
I guess, man--you're something
else, MICKEY.

                    CARTER
Tell me about it. This guy flew
over the cuckoo's nest.

MICKEY pours himself, DRE, and CARTER another drink.

                    MICKEY
I wish we we're getting more than
2.5 on this next job.

                    CARTER
That would be nice. But, damn,
man, be grateful, we're getting
plenty off this next job.

                    MICKEY
Come on, CARTER, you and I both
know that probably won't even last
a decade once we split it into
shares. This is my last job, and I
want to be straight for life. I
don't want to have to be a thief
                    (MORE)

                    MICKEY (cont'd)
any longer.

                    DRE
This is your last job?

                    MICKEY
Yep.

                    CARTER
If this is your last job, then
this is my last job. You're my
friend and you're my brother.
We've been through good, bad, and
ugly together so if you're calling
it quits then so am I.

                    DRE
Same here.

                    CARTER
So, what do you guys propose we
do? I mean, you're right, MICKEY,
we can't keep robbing banks. That
shit will catch up with us
eventually, so we should retire
after this job. But, 2.5 mill
between the three of us won't last
long at all.

                    MICKEY
I say we turn on BRODY. I say we
take all the loot, get out of
town, and never look back. We
sever ties with each other and go
our separate ways and live our
lives out peacefully.

                    DRE
I don't know, man, that sounds
pretty messed up. BRODY has been
good to us since day one. He's
gotten us to where we are today.
And, BRODY is the Boss. If he were
to find out what you just said
he'd have VITO and GERALD crucify
us, literally.

                    MICKEY
BRODY thinks he's a boss. He was
given his position. His money and
his power were not earned, they
were thrust upon him. He thinks
he's a god. To hell with BRODY.
                    (MORE)

                    MICKEY (cont'd)
Let's do the job, take the loot,
and go as far away from here as we
possibly can. Think of all we can
do with $25,000,000. We can live
with life and liberty without
having to keep pursuing happiness.
It's not like BRODY is going to
miss it. He has enough money to
last him 10 lifetimes.

DRE and CARTER contemplate what MICKEY has said.

                    CARTER
                (in agreement)
I agree, MICKEY. If we're gonna
retire after this job, why not
just take it all and be free? It's
not like BRODY is doing the work.
He's going to be sitting back in
his OFFICE, smoking a Cohiba while
we're putting our lives at
risk...and for what?! A 10 percent
cut?! No way, man. Let's do it,
MICKEY. I'm in.

                    DRE
                (contemplating)
Ah, fuck it. I'm in too.

                    MICKEY
Good. We deserve to be able to be
free, travel and enjoy ourselves.
If we're not living, then we're
dying. We should be able to do
this job independently with no
strings attached. Let's do what we
got to do and retire from this
shit for good. That is our gold!

                    CARTER
Damn it, MICKEY, you are one crazy
motherfucker.

                    MICKEY
                (very serious)
Yes. I am that I am.

                    DRE
We'll go out with the gold and the
glory. Hell, after this job we'll
be the talk of the town.

                         MICKEY
                    (with authority)
          We're already the talk of the
          town. Now, let's take it!
                    (with a great big
                     smile)
          Let's create CHAOS one last time.

                         CARTER
          Yes, sir, Mr. President! We shall
          Prevail!

MICKEY, DRE, and CARTER are like brothers...

DRE and CARTER are MICKEY'S only family.

All three are devoted to one another. Each of them is the
other's keeper...

                                        CUT TO:

EXT. BRODY'S HOUSE - CONTINUOUS

GERALD and VITO pull up to BRODY'S HOUSE. They walk up to
the door and are let in by BRODY himself.

                                        CUT TO:

INT. BRODY'S HOUSE - MOMENTS LATER

BRODY welcomes GERALD and VITO into his HOUSE. He shuts the
door behind them.

BRODY starts walking to his OFFICE.

                         BRODY
          Let's go to my OFFICE, boys.

GERALD and VITO follow BRODY to the OFFICE.

                                        CUT TO:

INT. BRODY'S OFFICE - CONTINUOUS

GERALD and VITO enter the OFFICE and BRODY shuts the door.

                         BRODY
          Have a seat, guys.

GERALD and VITO take a seat. BRODY goes behind his desk and
sits down.

                    BRODY
          So what's going on with you two?
          You boys get the job done for me?

                    GERALD
          Yeah, BRODY, we put them all on
          ice. You won't be hearing from
          them anymore.

                    BRODY
          Good. I'm glad to finally get rid
          of those little pricks. They had
          it coming to them.

BRODY reaches below his desk, and gives GERALD and VITO
$20,000 each.

                    BRODY
          Here you go, boys.

                    VITO
          I thought you were only giving us
          15 each?

                    BRODY
          Ah, you know me, I put a cherry on
          top, here and there. So, how's
          everything going with you two?

                    GERALD
          I can't complain, boss. Well, I
          could, but it wouldn't do me any
          good.

                    BRODY
          Ain't that the truth. What about
          you, VITO, everything straight
          with you and yours?

                    VITO
          Yeah, BRODY, I'm good. We got the
          job done and I'm paid, so
          everything is good in my book.

                    BRODY
              (smirking)
          Spoken like a true assassin.

VITO seems bothered.

                    VITO
              (concerned)
There is one thing that is
bothering me, though, BRODY.

                    BRODY
And what would that be, VITO?

                    VITO
It's about that job you got coming
up tomorrow. You know, the one you
gave MICKEY and them.--

                    GERALD
--Come on, man, leave that shit
alone.--

                    BRODY
--No, GERALD, let the man speak.
What is bothering you, VITO?--

                    VITO
--I just don't trust MICKEY. I
have this gut feeling that
something just ain't right. I
can't explain it, but the look on
his face when you told him about
that job just made me feel like he
is going to try to fuck you over.
I know they've done several jobs
for you, but I got a bad feeling
about this one.

                    BRODY
VITO, do I pay you to feel?

                    VITO
No, BRODY, you pay me to kill.

                    BRODY
Precisely. Now, I understand where
you are coming from. Human beings
are petty, depraved creatures.
They steal, lie, cheat, and
everything in-between. But, VITO
you must understand one thing; I'm
the Boss. I have eyes and ears,
everywhere, on everything. Nothing
gets by me. If somebody takes a
shit, I know what they ate the
night before.
              (lights a COHIBA
               and puffs it a
               few times)
                    (MORE)

                    BRODY (cont'd)
But, since you've brought your
concerns to my attention and
you're genuinely worried, I will
take your conjecture into
consideration.

                    VITO
I understand, BRODY, and like I
was saying I'm not trying to cast
doubt on what you do or how you do
it. You're my boss. You have my
respect, you have my loyalty. I
just don't want to see MICKEY get
over on you, that's all.

                    BRODY
              (puffing his
              COHIBA)
That's very thoughtful of you,
VITO. As I said, I will consider
what you have told me. Now, you
boys take your payment and go to
the STRIP-CLUB or something. You
boys have earned a much needed
break in my eyes. Get out of my
sight and go have some fun.

                    GERALD
All right, BRODY, we appreciate
it.

                    VITO
Thanks, BRODY. We'll see you
later.

GERALD and VITO get up from their seats. They start toward
the door to leave. As they are walking to the door, BRODY
picks up his phone and makes a mysterious call. GERALD and
VITO exit BRODY'S OFFICE and his HOUSE.

                                        FADE TO BLACK:

                                        CHAPTER TITLE
                                        APPEARANCE:

IV. THE METHOD TO MADNESS

                                        FADE IN:

INT. FRANKO'S OFFICE - EVENING

FRANKO examines MICKEY'S rap-sheet closely.

> DETECTIVE FRANKO
> (talking to
> himself/reading
> over MICKEY'S
> sheet)
> Let's see. MICKEY MONTANA: been
> charged with misdemeanor
> marijuana-possession, and felony
> assault. Did 2 years in state
> prison, is a college graduate, has
> bi-polar disorder--he's been
> committed to several mental
> institutions. Damn. Known
> accomplices: DRE FERRARA, and
> MICHAEL CARTER.

FRANKO gets on his computer and searches for DRE and
CARTER'S files. He prints off both of their rap-sheets and
examines them...

> DETECTIVE FRANKO
> (talking to
> himself)
> DRE FERRARA: misdemeanor marijuana
> possession, DUI, grand theft auto,
> 3 years in state prison. MICHAEL
> CARTER: misdemeanor marijuana
> possession, petty theft, assault
> on a police-officer, 2 years in
> state prison.

FRANKO contemplates to himself.

> DETECTIVE FRANKO
> (soliloquy)
> These have to be the guys. I
> wonder who is giving them the
> jobs? Must be someone who is
> pretty powerful, someone feared,
> someone respected. Could it be???

FRANKO proceeds to further examine the Police-Database. He
digs deeper...

> CUT TO:

INT. FRANKO'S OFFICE - LATER

FRANKO gets up from desk quickly, grabs his things and heads to the CHIEF'S OFFICE.

                                        CUT TO:

EXT. CHIEF'S OFFICE - MOMENTS LATER

FRANKO knocks at the closed door of the CHIEF'S OFFICE.

                    CHIEF BARNES
          Come on in...

FRANKO enters the CHIEF'S OFFICE.

                                        CUT TO:

INT. CHIEF'S OFFICE - CONTINUOUS

FRANKO takes a seat.

                    CHIEF BARNES
          What do you got for me, FRANKO?

                    DETECTIVE FRANKO
          Sir, I think I've found out who is
          committing the robberies.

                    CHIEF BARNES
          Enlighten me.

                    DETECTIVE FRANKO
          I have reason to believe that a
          man by the name of MICKEY MONTANA
          is the leader of the so-called:
          'ELITE'. He, DRE FERRARA, and
          MICHAEL CARTER are the ones
          perpetrating these robberies. I'm
          sure of it. I've got addresses for
          all three, and I'd like to get a
          search-warrant for MICKEY
          MONTANA'S HOUSE in COMPTON; I
          suspect he is the leader of 'THE
          ELITE'. Also, sir, I've checked
          the database, and I found that
          several AMBULANCES and several
          people were all reported missing
          the day after each heist 'THE
          ELITE' performed. Coincidentally,
          scorched AMBULANCES with burned
          bodies in the driver-seats are
                    (MORE)

                    DETECTIVE FRANKO (cont'd)
          being discovered throughout LA,
          left and right, every other month.
          An--

The CHIEF'S phone rings.

                    CHIEF BARNES
          --Hold on, FRANKO.

CHIEF BARNES answers his phone.

                    CHIEF BARNES
                (talking into the
                 phone)
          Hello?

The CHIEF listens for about 30 seconds.

                    CHIEF BARNES
                (talking into the
                 phone)
          --Not a problem, I'll take care of
          it.

THE CHIEF hangs up the phone and continues talking with
FRANKO.

                    CHIEF BARNES
          Damn, FRANKO. How did you find
          out this information so quickly?

                    DETECTIVE FRANKO
          Well, sir, it was pretty simple. I
          found a piece of hair in the BANK.
          I had it analyzed by my guy. And,
          MICKEY MONTANA is the guy who
          popped up. His known accomplices
          are DRE FERRARA and MICHAEL
          CARTER. And, I know it in my gut
          that these are our guys, sir.
          These guys are clean as can be.
          They never kill anyone on their
          jobs, except their getaway-DRIVER.
          Now, I've reported to you as you
          said. Where do we go from here?

                    CHIEF BARNES
          Well, FRANKO, it looks like you've
          actually been working. I want you
          to continue your investigation.
          Get me something substantive, and
          then I'll try to get you a warrant
                    (MORE)

                    CHIEF BARNES (cont'd)
          for MONTANA'S place.

                    DETECTIVE FRANKO
          All right, sir. But, there is one
          more thing.

                    CHIEF BARNES
          What's that?

                    DETECTIVE FRANKO
          I know who's giving them the jobs.

                    CHIEF BARNES
          Who would that be?

                    DETECTIVE FRANKO
          BRODY. I know we don't have
          anything on the guy, not even a
          last name or a picture. But I am
          certain it's him giving 'THE
          ELITE' their jobs.

                    CHIEF BARNES
          Okay, FRANKO. Since you're on the
          ball, I'll call the judge and have
          him provide with you with a
          warrant. I want you, POLANSKI and
          DUNN to head to MONTANA'S
          residence as soon as I get the
          approval from the judge.

                    DETECTIVE FRANKO
          All right, sir, you got it.

FRANKO exits the CHIEF'S OFFICE and heads back to his OFFICE
to wait on CHIEF BARNES' go ahead.

                                        CUT TO:

INT. FRANKO'S OFFICE - MOMENTS LATER

CHIEF BARNES walks into FRANKO'S OFFICE.

                    CHIEF BARNES
          I got the approval, you three are
          good to go.

                    DETECTIVE FRANKO
          All right, CHIEF, I'm on it.

FRANKO hops up from his desk and exits his OFFICE in search of OFFICER POLANSKI and OFFICER DUNN.

                                    CUT TO:

INT. POLICE-STATION - MOMENTS LATER

FRANKO finds OFFICER POLANSKI and OFFICER DUNN.

                    DETECTIVE FRANKO
          POLANSKI, DUNN. I need you two to
          come with me; CHIEF'S orders. I
          got a lead on 'THE ELITE' case. We
          gotta search-warrant for MICKEY
          MONTANA'S place.

                    POLANSKI
          Okay, FRANKO, not a problem. Let's
          go, DUNN.

                    DUNN
          All right, let's do it.

The two POLICE OFFICERS get up from their desks and follow DETECTIVE FRANKO out of the POLICE-STATION.

                                    CUT TO:

INT. STRIP-CLUB - EVENING

GERALD and VITO enter a STRIP-CLUB. The place is dark and somewhat crowded. There are older and younger men watching the dancers in a daze. Very exotic and beautiful women are strip-dancing. Club-music is playing in the background; GERALD and VITO take a seat at one of the stripper's areas.

                    VITO
          Damn, this was a pretty good idea,
          huh?

                    GERALD
          Yeah, it was. Kudos to BRODY. But
          if my wife finds out I've been
          here, she'll kill me.

                    VITO
          You'll be all right, man. Just
          enjoy yourself. Don't be so
          uptight.

>   GERALD
>   You're right, brother. I just need
>   to chill and appreciate the asses
>   and titties that are up in this
>   place.

>   VITO
>   Yes, brother, indeed.

>   CUT TO:

INT. STRIP-CLUB - MOMENTS LATER

Both GERALD and VITO pull out a stack of hundreds and throw
a few at the dancer they are watching.

>   GERALD
>   (laughing)
>   Here you go, girl, do something
>   for ya boy!

The dancer gets closer to VITO and GERALD. VITO is
absolutely amazed by her beauty.

>   VITO
>   (in a trance)
>   Damn, girl. You're the most
>   beautiful woman I've ever seen.

>   CHERRY
>   (talking to VITO
>   and giggling)
>   Thank you, Papi.

>   VITO
>   I have a few ideas of what I would
>   like to do with you.

>   GERALD
>   (jokingly)
>   Ah, damn, my boy done fell in love
>   with a stripper.

GERALD and VITO continue to serve the stripper twenties and
fifties. She keeps dancing in front of them quite sensually.
After a few more fifties are thrown she begins bouncing her
booty, this stuns both GERALD and VITO. But she is
seductively staring down VITO. After doing a few more moves,
the stripper leans close to VITO and whispers in his ear.

                         CHERRY
                    (whispering to
                    VITO)
          Meet me in the back. I want you in
          the VIP.

                         VITO
                    (to the stripper)
          Really? All right, let's do it.

She gets down from her platform, grabs VITO gently by the
hand and proceeds to take him to the VIP SECTION.

                         GERALD
                    (confused)
          Where you going, VITO?

                         VITO
                    (smiling)
          I don't know, man, but I'll be
          back when she's done with me.

                         GERALD
                    (laughing)
          All right, Brother, do what you
          gotta do.

The Stripper and VITO head to the VIP SECTION in the back of
the STRIP-CLUB. GERALD gets up and finds another beautiful
stripper to throw money at.

                                        CUT TO:

INT. VIP SECTION - MOMENTS LATER

The stripper sits VITO down and the two begin to chat while
she proceeds to give him a lap-dance.

                         CHERRY
          So what do you do for a living,
          Papi?

                         VITO
          Well, I'm really not at liberty to
          say.

                         CHERRY
                    (being sarcastic)
          Why, do you kill people or
          something?

                    VITO
                (serious)
          Well, as a matter of fact I do.

She continues dancing thinking VITO is joking.

                    CHERRY
                (very sensual, and
                using a sexy
                accent)
          Very funny, Papi. Really, what do
          you do?

                    VITO
          I just told you, baby. I'm a
          hitman.

She stops dancing, and looks at VITO with great interest. He
mistakes it for fear.

                    VITO
          Does that frighten you?

                    CHERRY
                (whispers to VITO
                while massaging
                his pelvic area)
          No, actually it turns me on.

                    VITO
          Really?

She starts dancing again.

                    CHERRY
                (curious as a cat)
          Yes, really. I've never met anyone
          that's killed someone before,
          especially for money.

                    VITO
                (captivated by
                CHERRY'S
                marvelous beauty)
          Well, now you have. I must say,
          I've never told anyone that
          before. You are the first person
          to know about my employment.

                    CHERRY
          My lips are sealed, Papacito. I
          can keep a secret. I'm good like
          that.

She begins grinding quite vigorously on VITO.

                    VITO
          Yes, you are, honey. Yes, you are.

                    CHERRY
          What is your name, Papi?

                    VITO
          My name is VITO. VITO TEDESCO.

                    CHERRY
          That's a very cool name. Are you
          Italian?

                    VITO
          I honestly don't know. I do know
          that some of my ancestors were
          Scots-Irish. I have some Indian in
          me as well. But I don't know about
          Italian. By the way, I love how
          you talk. You must be Hispanic,
          huh?

                    CHERRY
          Yes, I'm Columbian. Columbian
          girls do it best.

                    VITO
               (serious tone)
          I couldn't agree more.

The Stripper continues grinding on VITO, she begins rubbing
him while grinding on him. VITO proceeds to put some
hundreds in CHERRY'S thong as she dances.

                    VITO
          What's your name, baby?

                    CHERRY
          Well, my Stripper name is Cherry
          Lane. I shouldn't be telling you
          this, but you are just too damn
          sexy. My real name is Lupe
          Maloney.

                    VITO
          Lupe is a beautiful name. I like
          that and I like the name: CHERRY
          Lane.

                    CHERRY
          Well, thank you, Papi. You can
          call me CHERRY. I like that
          better.

                    VITO
          All right, whatever you say,
          sweetheart. I have a question for
          you.

                    CHERRY
          What would that be?

                    VITO
          Are you a lady trying to be a
          freak? Or are you a freak trying
          to be a lady?

                    CHERRY
               (giggling, still
                dancing)
          What kind of a question is that?

                    VITO
          It's a serious question. I need to
          know.

                    CHERRY
          Well, I guess I'm a freak trying
          to be a lady. Is that the answer
          you are looking for?

                    VITO
               (amazed)
          Yes, it is, darling. Yes, it is.

VITO pulls out five more hundreds and puts them in CHERRY'S
thong. She dances even harder on him.

                                        CUT TO:

INT. STRIP-CLUB - MOMENTS LATER

GERALD is enjoying himself, watching another stripper
perform. He sees a MAN walk in. GERALD glances at the MAN
without much thought and he just keeps watching the stripper
before him...

The MAN walks up to the RECEPTIONIST of the STRIP-CLUB.

                    TONY
               (talking to the
               RECEPTIONIST)
          Where is CHERRY?

                    STRIP-CLUB RECEPTIONIST
          She is in the VIP SECTION, TONY,
          how can I help you?

The MAN walks angrily toward the VIP section.

GERALD sees TONY walking toward the VIP SECTION, but he
thinks nothing of it.

                    STRIP-CLUB RECEPTIONIST
          Wait! You can't go back there!

                    TONY
               (aggressively)
          Watch me!

                    STRIP-CLUB RECEPTIONIST
          Security!

Two SECURITY GUARDS approach TONY.

As the two SECURITY GUARDS approach TONY, he pulls out a
pistol and shoots them dead. He proceeds to the VIP SECTION
with his gun in-hand.

                                        CUT TO:

GERALD hops up from the section he's in and moves toward the
VIP SECTION. GERALD realizes that VITO is in danger.

                    GERALD
          Oh, shit, VITO!!!

                                        CUT TO:

INT. VIP SECTION - MOMENTS LATER

CHERRY is still dancing on VITO. Suddenly TONY bursts
through the door of the VIP SECTION...

                    TONY
          You fucking whore!

                    CHERRY
          Aah! TONY, please, don't!

TONY punches CHERRY in the face, grabs her and then points
his gun at VITO...

> VITO
> Let her go, now!

TONY holds the gun to CHERRY'S head.

> TONY
> Or what, buddy?! Never bring fists
> to a gun-fight!

TONY has his finger on the trigger of the gun, and he is
about to squeeze...

VITO swiftly hops up. The weapon goes off. A bullet grazes
VITO, but he is able to grab the weapon, disarm TONY, and
protect CHERRY.

GERALD, after manuvering around, finally gets to the VIP
SECTION; the STRIP-CLUB was crowded with panicked folks who
were trying to get out...

> GERALD
> (shocked)
> VITO! You all right, brother?!

TONY is lying on his back. VITO points the gun at him.

> VITO
> I'm good, GERALD. He beat on this
> woman and tried to shoot me, but
> I'm good.

> GERALD
> (wide-eyed and
> very angry)
> Who the fuck do you think you
> are?! You tried to kill my
> brother?! I eat motherfuckers like
> you for breakfast, lunch, and
> dinner!

GERALD punches TONY several times...

> VITO
> It seems what we have here is a
> woman-beater. CHERRY, is this your
> husband?

> CHERRY
> (in great fear)
> Y-y-yes, he is...

                         VITO
          Does he beat on you?

                       CHERRY
                      (crying)
          Yes, he does!

                         VITO
          I suppose you won't mind if my
          friend and I beat his ass to a
          pulp really quick, will you?

                       CHERRY
                   (without even
                    thinking about it)
          Beat his ass!

VITO throws down TONY'S pistol. GERALD and VITO take it upon
themselves to brutally and viciously beat TONY till he's
black and blue. They kick him, punch him and stomp him;
GERALD and VITO nearly beat TONY to death, but they do not
kill him.

                                        CUT TO:

GERALD and VITO discontinue the beating.

VITO grabs CHERRY by her waist and kisses her. She hugs VITO
very tightly.

She lets him go, and he and GERALD exit the VIP SECTION.

                       GERALD
          Come on, VITO, we gotta dip, man!

CHERRY just stands there in awe.

                       CHERRY
                   (in reference to
                    VITO)
          My hero...Thank you...Mi Amor.

GERALD and VITO scramble to exit the STRIP-CLUB before the
cops arrive.

                                        CUT TO:

EXT. STRIP-CLUB - MOMENTS LATER

GERALD and VITO sprint to their CAR.

                    GERALD
               (sprinting
                alongside VITO)
Man, damn! If we don't find
trouble, it finds us!

                    VITO
               (sprinting but
                also smiling)
I don't think trouble found me,
GERALD, I think LOVE found me...

                    GERALD
               (laughing)
Damn, VITO, you really did fall in
Love with a Stripper!

They get in the 2012 YELLOW CHEVY CAMARO and speed off from
the STRIP-CLUB.

                              CUT TO:

EXT. POLICE-STATION - CONTINUOUS

FRANKO, DUNN, and POLANSKI run to a POLICE-CRUISER and enter
it.

                              CUT TO:

INT. POLICE-CRUISER - MOMENTS LATER

DETECTIVE FRANKO is in the passenger-seat, OFFICER POLANSKI
is in the back, and OFFICER DUNN is driving.

                 DETECTIVE FRANKO
               (readying his
                weapon)
All right, guys, we need to be
ready. We don't know what we're
going to find or face when we get
there, so let's be prepared.

                    DUNN
We got you, FRANKO.

DUNN pulls into an empty ALLEYWAY and stops the
POLICE-CRUISER.

                 DETECTIVE FRANKO
               (confused)
What the hell?

                         POLANSKI
               BRODY sends his regards...

POLANSKI pulls out his pistol and shoots FRANKO directly in
the back of the head.

DETECTIVE FRANKO'S blood and brains splatter all over the
front-window of the POLICE-CRUISER.

                                        CUT TO:

INT. POLICE-CRUISER - CONTINUOUS

                         POLANSKI
               That ought to teach him a lesson.

                                        CUT TO:

The two OFFICERS exit the POLICE-CRUISER.

                                        CUT TO:

EXT. ALLEYWAY - MOMENTS LATER

The two OFFICERS walk down the ALLEYWAY and are met by a
BLACK SUV. They enter the BLACK SUV and ride off from the
ALLEYWAY...

                                        CUT TO:

INT. AMBULANCE - DAY

MICKEY, DRE, CARTER, and their driver are parked across the
street from a BANK in an AMBULANCE. MICKEY, DRE, and CARTER
have on their PRESIDENTIAL ATTIRE and they have their
machine-guns ready.

                    MICKEY
               All right, guys, we have one shot
               at this. Now, let's get into
               character and take care of
               business.

                    DRE
               Okay, Mr. President, we are
               ready...

                         CARTER
          Mr. President, Mr. Clinton, this
          will be a mighty diplomatic
          success!

                         MICKEY
                    (commando-style)
          As Commander-in-Chief, I think
          it's time we enter the BANK and
          get those golden bars. Now, let's
          do this!

MICKEY, DRE, and CARTER exit the AMBULANCE.

                                        CUT TO:

EXT. BANK - MOMENTS LATER

They sprint toward the entrance of the BANK and enter.

Immediately after MICKEY, DRE, and CARTER enter the BANK,
shots are fired.

                                        CUT TO:

                                        2 MINUTES LATER

EXT. BANK - MOMENTS LATER

POLICE sirens are wailing, and POLICE VEHICLES begin
surrounding the BANK. MICKEY exits the BANK without the
loot, and without DRE and CARTER. DRE and CARTER are dead.

MICKEY is covered in blood, has multiple gunshot wounds, his
OBAMA-MASK is halfway ripped off his face. His clothes are
torn to shreds. He still has his weapon in his hands. MICKEY
is injured, shocked, distraught, and very pissed off.

                         MICKEY
                    (quietly talking
                     to himself)
          DRE, CARTER? How could this have
          happened?

POLICE have surrounded the BANK and MICKEY.

MICKEY is completely oblivious to what is occurring around
him. POLICEMAN 1 uses a megaphone to demand MICKEY'S
surrender...

                    POLICEMAN 1
          You are under arrest! Drop your
          weapon, put your hands above your
          head and get on the ground, or we
          will use deadly force!

MICKEY drops his weapon but he stays standing...

POLICEMAN 1 hands the megaphone to POLICEMAN 4.

POLICEMAN 1, POLICEMAN 2 and POLICEMAN 3 slowly approach
MICKEY with their guns drawn...

                    POLICEMAN 2
          Put your hands in the air right
          now, or we will put you down!

                    POLICEMAN 3
          Don't you fucking move!

MICKEY puts his hands in the air. The POLICEMEN get to
MICKEY. One of them attempts to grab him to cuff him.

When POLICEMAN 1 grabs MICKEY'S arm, he immediately reacts.

MICKEY elbows POLICEMAN 1 in the face and breaks his nose.

MICKEY kicks POLICEMAN 2 in the leg and breaks his knee
inwards.

Within a split-second MICKEY strikes POLICEMAN 3 and
snatches his weapon from him.

MICKEY takes the weapon and shoots both POLICEMAN 1 and
POLICEMAN 2 in the face. MICKEY picks up POLICEMAN 3 and
uses him as a human-shield...

                    POLICEMAN 4
                 (through the
                  speaker-phone)
          LET THE OFFICER GO NOW!!!

The hordes of POLICE are all yelling indistinctly.

                    MICKEY
                 (with vindication)
          So much for Amsterdam. This is for
          DRE and CARTER.

MICKEY points the gun to the head of POLICEMAN 3 and pulls
the trigger.

Immediately after killing POLICEMAN 3, MICKEY charges the POLICE and fires his weapon at them.

                    MICKEY
               (shouting)
          FREEDOM!

The POLICE shoot MICKEY several times. He takes shots to his body and continues running at the POLICE. A sniper shoots him in the chest. MICKEY finally falls to the ground, presumably dead.

The POLICEMEN run to their fellow OFFICERS aid. The three cops are dead, as is MICKEY. The scene is CHAOS.

                                        CUT TO:

INT. BRODY'S OFFICE - LATER

BRODY'S OFFICE-phone rings. He answers it. It's CHIEF BARNES on the other line...

                    BRODY
               (talking into the
                phone)
          Yes?

                    CHIEF BARNES
               (through the phone)
          We got MICKEY and his boys. Also,
          I personally handled a DETECTIVE
          that was on your trail. You have
          nothing to worry about, BRODY.

                    BRODY
               (talking into the
                phone)
          Good work, little brother.

BRODY BARNES hangs up the phone, stands up from his desk and fixes his tie...

                    BRODY
               (soliloquy)
          It is done...

                                        FADE TO BLACK:

                                        CHAPTER TITLE
                                        APPEARANCE:

V. REVENGE IS SWEETER

                                        FADE IN:

INT. HOSPITAL HALLWAY - NIGHT

Two DOCTORS in white lab coats are pushing a stretcher down
a HOSPITAL HALLWAY. There is a corpse on the stretcher. It
is the corpse of MICKEY MONTANA in a black body-bag.

                    DOCTOR 1
          --I heard this guy was a bad-ass.
          He tried to rob a BANK, and ended
          up killing 6 security guards and 3
          cops by himself. He had two guys
          with him. They're deader than
          hell, too. I saw on the news that
          the security guards killed this
          guy's partners when they entered
          the BANK, and then he went
          ape-shit.

                    DOCTOR 2
          Are you serious?

                    DOCTOR 1
          Yeah. This guy took several
          bullets before going down. One
          tough son-of-a-bitch, huh?

                    DOCTOR 2
          Holy Shit.

                    DOCTOR 1
          That's what I said when I found
          out about it.

The two DOCTORS push the stretcher with the body-bag through
two sets of doors, and then the DOCTORS enter an EXAMINATION
ROOM...

                                        CUT TO:

INT. EXAMINATION ROOM - MOMENTS LATER

A MEDICAL-EXAMINER is already in the EXAMINATION ROOM
examining a corpse as the DOCTORS bring in the stretcher
with the body-bag.

                    MEDICAL-EXAMINER
          Hey, guys.

She sees the incoming body-bag.

                    MEDICAL-EXAMINER
          Come on, you got another one for
          me?

                    DOCTOR 2
          Yeah, but this one is special.

                    MEDICAL-EXAMINER
          How's that?

                    DOCTOR 1
          He's the bank robber with the
          OBAMA-MASK.

                    MEDICAL-EXAMINER
               (stressed)
          I'm almost done with my shift.
          Can't he wait till tomorrow?

                    DOCTOR 1
          Nope. We need a full autopsy and
          report. FBI orders.

                    MEDICAL-EXAMINER
               (pissed and sassy)
          Whatever. I'll get him done as
          soon as I can...

The two DOCTOR'S exit the EXAMINATION ROOM. The
MEDICAL-EXAMINER, stops examining the body in front of her.
She glances at the body-bag that has MICKEY inside of it and
gets curious.

                              CUT TO:

The MEDICAL-EXAMINER walks over to the body-bag.

The MEDICAL-EXAMINER slowly unzips the body-bag, revealing
MICKEY MONTANA. He is bloodied and lifeless.

                              CUT TO:

MICKEY'S OBAMA-MASK is half-way torn off of his face; half
of his face is showing and the other half of his face is
covered with the OBAMA-MASK. He is still in his PRESIDENTIAL
ATTIRE; his outfit is torn up.

The MEDICAL-EXAMINER starts to remove MICKEY'S OBAMA-MASK.
As soon as she touches MICKEY'S MASK, his eyes shoot open
and he grabs the MEDICAL-EXAMINER by the arm and breaks her
arm...

                         MICKEY
                    (angered)
               Where is BRODY?!

                         MEDICAL-EXAMINER
                    (in great pain)
               I-I-I don't know who BRODY is!
               You're supposed to be dead!

                         MICKEY
                    (rips the
                    OBAMA-MASK off of
                    his face)
               Not today, Bitch!

MICKEY grabs the MEDICAL-EXAMINER by the neck and breaks her
neck. He exits the HOSPITAL through the window of the
EXAMINATION ROOM...

                                        CUT TO:

INT. HOSPITAL PARKING-LOT - MOMENTS LATER

MICKEY finds a VEHICLE in the HOSPITAL PARKING-LOT. He
breaks the driver-side window of the VEHICLE and gets inside
of it. He hot-wires the VEHICLE and then drives off...

                                        CUT TO:

EXT. SAFE-HOUSE - LATER

MICKEY pulls up to a SAFE-HOUSE. He exits the VEHICLE and
then enters SAFE-HOUSE...

                                        CUT TO:

INT. SAFE-HOUSE - MOMENTS LATER

In the SAFE-HOUSE are many weapons. It is MICKEY'S secret
SAFE-HOUSE. He walks around looking at his weapons. He
selects only a few: a G-18 pistol and two blades.

                         MICKEY
                    (grabbing weapons)
               These should see me through...

He grabs a holster for his G-18 and loads the weapon with a
full clip. He then puts the gun in the holster.

He also grabs two knife-holders for his blades; one attaches

to his belt, and the other straps to his ankle. He puts the
blades in the knife-holders. He has one blade on his belt
and he has the other stapped to his ankle.

MICKEY does not change clothing, and he still has on his
PRESIDENTIAL ATTIRE; minus his OBAMA-MASK...

MICKEY exits the SAFE-HOUSE with his weapons.

                                        CUT TO:

EXT. SAFE-HOUSE - MOMENTS LATER

MICKEY enters the VEHICLE he stole from the HOSPITAL. He
takes off from the SAFE-HOUSE...

                                        CUT TO:

EXT. BRODY'S HOUSE - LATER

MICKEY pulls up near BRODY'S HOUSE and stops. He readies his
G-18.

MICKEY exits the VEHICLE, and sneaks toward BRODY'S HOUSE.

MICKEY jumps the gate. He then walks slowly toward the front
of BRODY'S HOUSE...

MICKEY looks right into the surveillance-cameras.

                    MICKEY
                 (angered)
            BRODY!!! Get your ass out here,
            right now!!! You and I have
            unfinished business!

                                        CUT TO:

INT. BRODY'S OFFICE - CONTINUOUS

BRODY is sitting at his OFFICE-desk looking into his
surveillance-monitors. VITO and GERALD are there with
BRODY...

BRODY sees MICKEY on the surveillance-monitors.

                    BRODY
                 (startled)
            What the hell? Impossible! VITO,
            GERALD, go take his ass out!

                    GERALD
          You got it, Boss...

VITO and GERALD exit BRODY'S HOUSE, cautiously, with their
guns drawn.

EXT. BRODY'S HOUSE - MOMENTS LATER

VITO and GERALD confront MICKEY.

MICKEY backs up as GERALD and VITO walk out...

                    MICKEY
          Where is BRODY?!

                    GERALD
          MICKEY, you've fucked up.

                    MICKEY
          My beef is not with you two. I
          only want BRODY, that's it. I
          don't want to have to put you guys
          down, but I will if I must.

                    VITO
          I don't think you're in any
          position to make threats. It's
          time for you to really die.

VITO and GERALD point their weapons at MICKEY.

                    MICKEY
                (roaring)
          NO!!!

MICKEY immediately points his G-18 at GERALD and unloads the
clip on him, killing GERALD on the spot...

                    VITO
                (fumbling his
                 weapon)
          GERALD!!!

                                        CUT TO:

MICKEY throws his gun down and starts running toward VITO.

VITO gains control of his weapon, and shoots MICKEY twice in
the chest...

MICKEY doesn't stop.

Within seconds, MICKEY pulls the blade from off of his belt and stabs VITO directly in the forehead. VITO and GERALD are both dead at BRODY'S doorstep.

MICKEY is severely wounded. He picks up GERALD's gun and kicks BRODY'S door down. MICKEY enters BRODY'S HOUSE with the firearm in-hand.

                                        CUT TO:

INT. BRODY'S HOUSE - MOMENTS LATER

                    MICKEY
                (greatly angered)
            Where are you, you son of a
            bitch?! Get out here! I've killed
            your dogs. Now it's your turn!

                                        CUT TO:

BRODY exits his OFFICE and proceeds to enter the living-room of his HOUSE. He walks toward MICKEY.

                    BRODY
            Hello, MICKEY...

                                        CUT TO:

MICKEY is pointing the firearm at BRODY.

                    MICKEY
            You tried to have me killed. You
            killed DRE! You killed CARTER!!!

                                        CUT TO:

BRODY is inching closer to MICKEY. BRODY stops and stands ready to battle.

                    BRODY
            I killed no one. My hands are
            clean.

                    MICKEY
            Your job, your plan!!! You set us
            up, you piece of shit!!!

                    BRODY
                (assertive and
                 very
                 condescending)
            Yes, I did, my boy. Nothing
            happens around here without my
                    (MORE)

                         BRODY (cont'd)
say. There were no Gold-Bars,
MICKEY...
            (laughs)
...I wipe my ass with 25 million.
I didn't need the Gold. I already
have more Gold than I know what to
do with. I just needed you to take
a fall. And you did fall. Yet,
here you are, and you survived the
CHAOS--You want to know something,
son? You've always been
persistent. It's your greatest
trait. But, you're also naive. You
think you can just walk in here
and take me out? If you want to
take my life, you'll have to do it
the old fashion way. I'm not
armed. Put down the weapon. You
want to kill me? You think coming
here to try to kill me will redeem
you, or DRE, or CARTER? I'm not
afraid of you. I own all the
bankers, I own all the lawyers, I
own all the politicians and police
this side of the Mississippi. And,
boy, you better believe that I own
you, too. I made you. Without me,
you are nothing. You killed
everybody that I sent at you.
Let's see how you fair against me.

                    MICKEY
You do a lot of talking for a dead
man.

                                   CUT TO:

MICKEY puts down the firearm. He runs toward BRODY with
great fury and ferocity.

He punches BRODY. BRODY takes the punches, unharmed.

                                   CUT TO:

BRODY grabs MICKEY by the neck, picks him up off of his feet
like a feather and throws him like a football, right into a
wall; the wall craters.

                                   CUT TO:

MICKEY lies on the ground, spitting blood. He is in
soul-crushing pain.

CUT TO:

BRODY slowly walks toward MICKEY in an intimidating and
physically-imposing fashion.

                    BRODY
               (with tremendous
               authority)
          What did you expect? You were
          going to betray me, and get away
          with it? NO! Remember, MICKEY, I
          know what you will do, before you
          do it. I can read you like a book.
          You were planning on crossing me,
          so, yes, I set you up. Obviously,
          you didn't die, so I'll just have
          to finish you off myself!

MICKEY takes another punch at BRODY and he blocks it.

                    MICKEY
               (shocked)
          AHHH!!!

BRODY kicks MICKEY in the chest.

MICKEY falls backward and lands on his back.

                    BRODY
          Anger has consumed you! Fear is in
          your eyes!!!

BRODY stands over MICKEY and strikes him in the face several
times. He subsequently elbows MICKEY in the face.

MICKEY gets up in great pain and continues to try and fight
BRODY to no avail. MICKEY continues to throw punches and
BRODY either dodges or blocks them, or he is not hurt by
them.

BRODY picks up MICKEY by the neck again and slams him into a
wall. BRODY holds MICKEY against the wall. MICKEY tries to
break free, but he cannot.

                    BRODY
               (intimidating)
          You think this will end in your
          victory? You think anger is your
          ally? Anger is merely an
          expression of fear; you fear me,
          my boy. You are angry simply
          because you fear me! Now, it is
          time for you to experience true
                    (MORE)

BRODY (cont'd)
fear!!!

BRODY, while grabbing MICKEY by the throat and pressing him
against the wall with his left-hand, furiously and rapidly
punches MICKEY in the body with his right-hand.

BRODY is strong as an ox. He lets go of MICKEY.

MICKEY falls to the ground.

MICKEY tries to get up once more and fight BRODY, but BRODY
elbows MICKEY in the face.

MICKEY is down, unable to fight BRODY any longer. BRODY
effortlessly picks MICKEY up, and throws him through the
living-room window. MICKEY lands outside in the yard.

BRODY exits his HOUSE through the door-way...

CUT TO:

EXT. BRODY'S HOUSE - MOMENTS LATER

BRODY walks toward MICKEY. He steps over the corpses of VITO
and GERALD.

BRODY
(assertive)
I built you up! Now, I will
destroy you!

CUT TO:

MICKEY gets up, and keeps punching BRODY in the face and
chest. BRODY takes the punches with ease. MICKEY backs up in
frustration; he is in great pain and he seemingly cannot
harm BRODY.

MICKEY
(swinging at BRODY)
Ahhh!!!

MICKEY punches BRODY in the face three more times and BRODY
is barely affected.

MICKEY throws another punch and BRODY catches his fist
mid-swing and headbutts MICKEY.

MICKEY falls down to the ground again.

CUT TO:

                    BRODY
               (intimidating)
     MICKEY, I'm impervious to your
     anger, and I am the cause of your
     fear. You are a petty little
     being; I am a GOD!!! Look at you!
     You think you're a hero, you
     little-shit? You think you can
     have redemption by killing me? No.
     No. No...I could crush you like a
     bug right now. You are merely an
     ant to a boot. Nothing more,
     nothing less. You're all alone;
     you have nothing left to fight
     for...

MICKEY is down on the ground in severe pain. He is
bleeding-out severely.

                    MICKEY
               (saddened)
     DRE...CARTER...

MICKEY stands tall, and punches at BRODY with every ounce of
energy he has.

                    MICKEY
               (swinging at BRODY)
     You've taken everything from me!!!

BRODY dodges MICKEY'S punches again and again.

                    BRODY
     Your punches are a practice in
     futility. Tonight you shall die by
     my hands!

BRODY slowly walks toward MICKEY. He grabs him by the neck
and picks him up off of his feet once more.

                    MICKEY
               (barely able to
                speak)
     You think you're so high and
     mighty?

                    BRODY
               (arrogantly)
     Yes, MICKEY, I do actually...

                    MICKEY
     You want to know the difference
     between you and me?

                  BRODY
          What's the difference, you
          little-shit?

                  MICKEY
          I'm still armed!

MICKEY swiftly reaches down to the knife-holder that is
strapped around his ankle and he pulls his blade. MICKEY
takes the blade and stabs BRODY under the chin.

BRODY, in shock, releases MICKEY.

                          CUT TO:

Faster than a bullet, MONTANA comes around with a
round-house kick right beneath BRODY'S chin where the knife
is, sending the blade directly into his brain.

                          CUT TO:

MICKEY kneels to the ground in pain. BRODY grabs his neck.
His blood is squirting everywhere. BRODY tries to pull the
knife out, but he cannot. He collapses to the ground, and
speaks his last words...

                  BRODY
             (choking on his
             own blood)
          I will see you in Hell, MICKEY!

MICKEY walks up to VITO'S corpse, picks up VITO'S gun and
walks back over to BRODY.

He points the weapon at BRODY. BRODY is barely alive, yet
still aware and functional, looking at MICKEY.

                  MICKEY
          This is for DRE. This is for
          CARTER. This is for me. Give
          Lucifer my regards...

MICKEY unloads the weapon on BRODY. He fires several shots
into his chest, and one directly into his forehead.

After shooting BRODY, MICKEY collapses to the ground.

BRODY is dead. MICKEY is apparently dead as well.

                          CUT TO:

INT. AMSTERDAM COFFEE SHOP - DAY

A MAN is sitting in an AMSTERDAM COFFEE SHOP, at a booth by
himself, smoking a joint. He has on a white V-neck shirt, a
lenghty black-jacket, and a black fedora. He has very long
dark hair and he also has a lengthy beard and mustache. We
do not see the top part of his face, only his hands and
mouth as he smokes the joint. He takes a big puff off of the
joint and subsequently puts it out in an ash-tray.

THE MAN walks up to the CASHIER of the COFFEE SHOP.

                    THE MAN
          Can I have 2 more grams of the O.G
          Kush and three of your
          space-cakes, please?

                    CASHIER
               (flirtatious)
          Will that be all for you, sir?
               (winks at THE MAN)
          You can have more...

                    THE MAN
          Yes, that will be all...

                    CASHIER
          That'll be 66 euros...

THE MAN pulls out his wallet, and gives the CASHIER the
money. She hands him the space-cakes and the two grams of
marijuana in a brown paper bag.

                    THE MAN
          Thanks.

                                        CUT TO:

The MAN takes his bag of purchases and puts his wallet back
in his pocket...

                    CASHIER
          The space-cakes are pretty sweet
          today. I hope you enjoy them...

The MAN smiles at the CASHIER.

                    THE MAN
               (with catharsis
                and appreciation)
          The Revenge is sweeter.

                        CASHIER
                      (confused)
            Huh???

                                          CUT TO:

THE MAN, with his bag of goods, smoothly walks toward the
exit of the COFFEE SHOP.

As he turns to leave the COFFEE SHOP his face is revealed:
it is MICKEY MONTANA, alive and well.

                                          CUT TO:

EXT. AMSTERDAM STREET - MOMENTS LATER

MICKEY still walks...

He moves along a busy AMSTERDAM STREET; he almost floats.
His jacket flails in the wind. He walks as the wind blows;
free at last...

                                          FADE OUT.

ORGANIZED CHAOS CONTINUED

by

Brandon S. Todd

Brandon S. Todd
820 North Flint St.
Lincolnton, NC 28092
704-501-6135
brandonstodd@abbey.bac.edu

FOA

FADE IN:

EXT. BAGHDAD, IRAQ - EVENING

                                    YEAR: 2003

The US has invaded IRAQ, in what is being called: 'Operation
Iraqi Freedom'

SADDAM HUSSEIN is facing abdication. Due to the offensive by
The United States, SADDAM'S Regime is falling apart. IRAQ is
destabilizing quite rapidly...

Fire and Death have consumed the failed nation-state...

                                    FADE TO BLACK:

                                    CHAPTER TITLE
                                    APPEARANCE:

I. CREATORS OF CHAOS

                                    FADE IN:

EXT. BAGHDAD - ROOF-TOP - CONTINUOUS

A MAN IN BLACK is standing on a ROOF-TOP in the middle of
war-torn BAGHDAD; gun-shots and explosions can be heard
going off throughout the ravaged city.

THE MAN IN BLACK is wearing a black mask; his face is
completely hidden. His attire is literally all-black, from
head-to-toe....

The black mask he is wearing is unique, and it is made of
Graphene fibers; it is very durable. The mask can withstand
a straight gun-shot from point-blank range. It has tinted
lenses, and the mask is strictly used by THE MAN IN BLACK
for tactical purposes, protection, as well as to conceal his
identity...

THE MAN IN BLACK is preparing a Dragunov SVU Sniper-Rifle...

                                    CUT TO:

Two of SADDAM'S highest ranking GENERALS are in the vicinity
of THE MAN IN BLACK. They are his targets...

GENERAL #1 is leaving a COMPOUND in a LIMO. He has no
security with him...

GENERAL #2 is inside the COMPOUND under the protection of
many ARMED GUARDS...

                                    CUT TO:

INT. GENERAL #1'S LIMO - CONTINUOUS

GENERAL #1 is relaxing in the LIMO, smoking a cigar,
listening to some Iraqi tunes...

The GENERAL rolls down the window that is between him and
his DRIVER...

                    GENERAL #1
                (speaking Arabic
                  to DRIVER)
            Cut the Music up!

                    GENERAL #1'S DRIVER
                (speaking Arabic)
            Yes, Sir, GENERAL!

GENERAL #1'S DRIVER cranks the music way up...

The GENERAL rolls the window back up.

                                    CUT TO:

INT. THE COMPOUND - CONTINUOUS

The COMPOUND in which GENERAL #2 is located is across from
the building THE MAN IN BLACK is at.

GENERAL #2 is snorting cocaine and enjoying himself...

The COMPOUND is not very secure; it is old and raggedy.
Also, the COMPOUND is not big; it is only 3 stories high,
with limited square-footage...

The COMPOUND is surrounded by, and filled with, ARMED
GUARDS...

                                    CUT TO:

EXT. BAGHDAD - ROOF-TOP - CONTINUOUS

THE MAN IN BLACK is looking through the scope of his
Sniper-Rifle, examining the LIMO...

He hunts his prey with great focus.

                                        CUT TO:

Under his mask, he has a comms-device in his ear.

                        THE MAN IN BLACK
                    (talking into
                     comms-device in
                     his ear)
            I have located both targets. Shall
            I proceed?

                            VOICE
                    (talking through
                     the comms)
            Yes, you may proceed.

THE MAN IN BLACK, being nearly 80-yards from the target,
puts his eye to the scope once more, and within a split
second he takes the shot...

                                        CUT TO:

The LIMO isn't moving very fast, so it's like shooting a
fish in a barrel for THE MAN IN BLACK. He is a superb
marksman...

                                        CUT TO:

INT. GENERAL #1'S LIMO - MOMENTS LATER

The bullet crashes through the back window of the LIMO, and
hits GENERAL #1 right in the back of the head. The shot
basically blows the GENERAL'S head clean-off...

                                        CUT TO:

The DRIVER hears the shot and immediately stops the LIMO and
cuts the music off...

The DRIVER turns around and sees the GENERAL'S headless
body.

                        GENERAL #1'S DRIVER
                    (speaking Arabic)
            HOLY HELL!!!

The GENERAL'S DRIVER gets out of the LIMO and runs away as
fast as he can...

THE MAN IN BLACK does not kill GENERAL #1'S DRIVER.

                                        CUT TO:

EXT. ROOF-TOP - CONTINUOUS

THE MAN IN BLACK throws his Dragunov SUV down, and picks up
a ARMSEL STRIKER semi-automatic 12-gauge Shotgun. The
shotgun has a sling, a pistol-grip and a 12-round rotating
cylinder, among other features...

THE MAN IN BLACK backs up several steps, and then proceeds
to do a jolt-sprint, and jumps from The ROOF-TOP...

The ROOF-TOP of the building he is jumping from is 6 stories
high. The COMPOUND he is jumping to is only 3 stories
high...

                                        CUT TO:

The drop is about 35 feet. It looks like THE MAN IN BLACK is
almost flying...

THE MAN IN BLACK shoots his shotgun in mid-air and blasts
open a window of GENERAL #2's COMPOUND. The shadowy figure
tactically enters the COMPOUND, performing a parkour-type
landing. He is prepared to kill...

                                        CUT TO:

INT. THE COMPOUND - MOMENTS LATER

The COMPOUND is filled with ARMED GUARDS; 22 to be exact.

About 20 more GUARDS are on the outside of the COMPOUND.

As soon as MICHAEL enters through the window, he shoots 5 of
the GUARDS with his shotgun, killing them instantly; each of
the GUARDS goes flying off their feet...

                                        CUT TO:

5 more GUARDS are guarding the door of the GENERAL'S
OFFICE...

THE MAN IN BLACK quickly straps the shotgun to his back and
sprints toward the GUARDS. The shadowy figure pulls a knife
as he runs toward the GUARDS. THE MAN IN BLACK moves quick
as lightning; in a few swift motions, using his knife, he
kills the other 5 GUARDS...

THE MAN IN BLACK puts the knife back in its sheath.

                                        CUT TO:

THE MAN IN BLACK walks up to the door of the GENERAL'S OFFICE, and puts his ear to the closed OFFICE-door...

He then pulls his shotgun from off of his back.

                              CUT TO:

THE MAN IN BLACK shoots a hole in the ceiling with his ARMSEL STRIKER shotgun and then he drops the weapon.

The shadowy figure jumps through the hole in the ceiling...

THE MAN IN BLACK crawls through the ceiling-infrastructure, and moves to the area right above the GENERAL'S OFFICE.

                              CUT TO:

INT. GENERAL #2'S OFFICE - CONTINUOUS

12 ARMED GUARDS are all nervously standing guard in the front of GENERAL #2 with their AK-47's pointed at the door...

                              CUT TO:

The GENERAL is distraught...

                    GENERAL #2
                  (speaking Arabic)
              Men! Prepare to fire!

Gripping their AK-47's, the GUARDS, speaking Arabic, shout: "Yes, Sir!"

                              CUT TO:

THE MAN IN BLACK, still in the ceiling-infrastructure, quickly busts a hole in the ceiling, and throws a flash-bang grenade into the OFFICE...

                              CUT TO:

The flash-bang grenade explodes and stuns the 12 GUARDS and the GENERAL...

                              CUT TO:

THE MAN IN BLACK jumps through the ceiling into the GENERAL'S OFFICE; he pulls his silenced-pistol, and shoots 7 of the GUARDS in the head with terrific precision...

He puts his silenced-pistol back in its holster and he pulls his knife with great quickness...

THE MAN IN BLACK runs up on 4 of the remaining GUARDS, who are still stunned, and in a couple quick motions he slices the GUARD'S throats like butter; they all suffocate on their own blood...

One GUARD remains.

                              CUT TO:

THE MAN IN BLACK lunges at the last GUARD, and grabs him by neck...

THE MAN IN BLACK picks the GUARD up off of his feet, slams him against the wall and then stabs him with awesome power...

The knife is holding the GUARD against the wall. He shakes as he hangs there and dies within a couple seconds...

                              CUT TO:

The GENERAL, hiding behind his desk, pulls his pistol from his desk-drawer...

The GENERAL jumps up from his hiding-spot and shoots three bullets right into the back of THE MAN IN BLACK...

THE MAN IN BLACK doesn't even have a vest on, and, yet, he takes the bullets with ease; he is barely affected...

THE MAN IN BLACK turns around after taking the shots like they were nothing.

                              CUT TO:

The GENERAL is wide-eyed and scared to death.

                    GENERAL #2
                 (consumed by fear
                  and in awe)
              W-w-who are you???

THE MAN IN BLACK takes off his mask and drops it on the floor, revealing the face of a unassuming, handsome, bearded MAN with bright sky-blue eyes and lengthy, silky blonde hair...

                    THE MAN IN BLACK
              I'm just a man on a mission.

CUT TO:

THE MAN IN BLACK takes his knife from the GUARD'S hanging body and throws it at the GENERAL, hitting him square in the right-eye...

The GENERAL falls back, shakes in shock and dies...

> THE MAN IN BLACK
> (touching his ear,
> talking into his
> comms)
> IT IS DONE.

> VOICE
> (through the comms)
> Good. Return to Base.

> THE MAN IN BLACK
> (talking into
> comms)
> Will do.

CUT TO:

INT. COMPOUND - MOMENTS LATER

A horde of GUARDS have entered the COMPOUND, and they are running to the GENERAL'S OFFICE to attack THE MAN IN BLACK.

The main-door to the OFFICE is still closed.

CUT TO:

INT. GENERAL #2'S OFFICE - CONTINUOUS

THE MAN IN BLACK has 4 sticky-bombs. The bombs are miniature explosive devices.

THE MAN IN BLACK throws a sticky-bomb on each wall of the GENERAL'S OFFICE; the bombs have blinking red-lights...

CUT TO:

The shadowy figure, THE MAN IN BLACK, vanishes from the COMPOUND...

He vanishes like the wind...

CUT TO:

EXT. GENERAL #2'S OFFICE - MOMENTS LATER

The other GUARDS fearfully surround the OFFICE door with their guns locked and loaded.

                                    CUT TO:

The three-leading GUARDS burst open the OFFICE door...

                                    CUT TO:

EXT. BAGHDAD STREET - CONTINUOUS

THE MAN IN BLACK, looking like a shadow, is walking calmly down the BAGHDAD STREET.

                                    CUT TO:

EXT. GENERAL #2'S OFFICE - MOMENTS LATER

The three-leading GUARDS proceed to enter the OFFICE...

                                    CUT TO:

EXT. BAGHDAD STREET - CONTINUOUS

THE MAN IN BLACK has a detonator in his hands.

As he is walking, he pushes the button on the detonator...

                                    CUT TO:

INT. GENERAL #2'S OFFICE - CONTINUOUS

After the three-leading GUARDS enter the OFFICE they hear: "Beep. Beep. BEEP."

With the third beep the sticky-bombs detonate, causing a fierce explosion.

Fire engulfs all the other remaining GUARDS and the COMPOUND itself. No one survives THE MAN IN BLACK.

                                    CUT TO:

EXT. BAGHDAD STREET - MOMENTS LATER

THE MAN IN BLACK moves away from the burning COMPOUND like a
ghost; unseen and unheard.

He walks up to a crappy, abandoned, yet still functioning
IRAQI POLICE VEHICLE. He breaks the driver-side window, and
enters the IRAQI POLICE VEHICLE, starts it and proceeds to
drive off from the CHAOS he created...

THE MAN IN BLACK is ghostly.

He is deadly. He is dangerous. He is: MICHAEL TEDESCO...

                                   CUT TO:

EXT. CITY STREET - MORNING

                                   YEAR: 2012

THREE AGENTS are riding down a CITY STREET in a BLACK SUV...

There is a fourth man in the BLACK SUV. He is the DRIVER.

                    AGENT ORANGE
                 (to the DRIVER)
               Be ready to take-off in 20
               minutes. That's all the time we
               need.

                    DRIVER
               Yes, sir, Boss!

                                   CUT TO:

INT. BLACK SUV - MOMENTS LATER

The THREE AGENTS riding in the BLACK SUV are readying
weapons and ammunition. They are also preparing grappling
and roping supplies for zip-lines...

                                   CUT TO:

EXT. ABANDON BUILDING - MOMENTS LATER

After pulling up to an ABANDONED BUILDING, directly across
from a government-building, AGENT KIMBO ORANGE, AGENT RAY
SMITH and AGENT CARL WHITE exit the BLACK SUV; they rush
into the ABANDONED BUILDING...

They are carrying their roping supplies, ammo and guns...

The ABANDONED BUILDING is 7 stories, and the
government-building across from it, the DEA BUILDING, is
only 4 stories. The government-building is The DEA HQ.

AGENT ORANGE'S DRIVER drives the BLACK SUV across the street
and parks it right in front of the DEA BUILDING...

The AGENTS are dressed to kill...

They are wearing suits: black blazers, white button-up
shirts, black pants. Their outfits match with the exception
of their ties.

AGENT WHITE is wearing a white tie with a black-bandana
themed design. AGENT SMITH is wearing a black tie with a
white-bandana themed design. AGENT ORANGE is wearing a
solid-orange tie; it is one of AGENT ORANGE'S theatrical
signatures to wear an orange tie...

AGENT ORANGE has hair the color of tangerines. He is pale as
a ghost. He has glowing lime-green eyes. AGENT ORANGE has
Death in his eyes.

                                        CUT TO:

INT. STAIRWELL - MOMENTS LATER

AGENT ORANGE is leading WHITE and SMITH up the STAIRWELL of
the ABANDONED BUILDING. They are sprinting up the STAIRWELL.

AGENT WHITE and AGENT SMITH are entirely loyal to AGENT
ORANGE. They kill for him. They would die for him...

The three AGENTS reach THE 7TH FLOOR of the ABANDONED
BUILDING...

                                        CUT TO:

INT. THE 7TH FLOOR - CONTINUOUS

The AGENTS walk up to a set of windows on THE 7TH FLOOR.

AGENT ORANGE pulls a metallic-device from his pocket. It is
filled with cocaine. The device allows him to snort coke
on-the-go.

                        AGENT ORANGE
                    (snorts coke)
            Guys, we're about to change The
            World...then we're going to take
                        (MORE)

                         AGENT ORANGE (cont'd)
          it over...
                    (smiling)
          ...The World is Ours...

                         AGENT SMITH
                    (placing a
                    100-round drum in
                    a Tommy-Gun)
          Yes, Sir, indeed.

                         AGENT WHITE
                    (placing a
                    100-round drum in
                    a Tommy-Gun)
          Those fuckers are dead-meat...

AGENT ORANGE snorts coke a couple of more times in both
nostrils, using his metallic-device. He then puts the
cocaine-filled device back in his pocket...

The AGENTS are preparing to create CHAOS.

                                        CUT TO:

INT. THE 7TH FLOOR - MOMENTS LATER

AGENT ORANGE, SMITH, and WHITE break 3 windows, and shoot
grappling hooks with rope, across the street, onto the roof
of The DEA BUILDING.

                                        CUT TO:

EXT. ABANDONED BUILDING - MOMENTS LATER

The AGENTS glide over on their zip-lines with ease;
undetected, unseen, and unexpected...

                                        CUT TO:

EXT. DEA BUILDING ROOF - MOMENTS LATER

After successfully landing on the DEA BUILDING ROOF, SMITH
cuts wires in a fuse-box, and, in turn, shuts down the
alarm-system of the BUILDING. He then proceeds to disable
the camera-system of the DEA BUILDING...

AGENT ORANGE knows the building like the back of his hand.
He, SMITH, and WHITE are still DEA AGENT'S. They're simply
RENEGADE, and totally corrupt.

ORANGE, SMITH, and WHITE were once superlative AGENTS till they were corrupted by money, drugs, and power...

                                        CUT TO:

There is a glass section of the roof. AGENT ORANGE and AGENT WHITE walk up to the glass and shoot it out with their pistols. ORANGE jumps down into the DEA BUILDING, using his rope. He swings on to the top floor, gunning down 7 people in the process...

                                        CUT TO:

INT. DEA BUILDING - CONTINUOUS

SMITH and WHITE follow AGENT ORANGE into the DEA BUILDING...

ORANGE has only a couple of pistols on him. SMITH and WHITE each have pistols, and they have Tommy-Guns with 100 round-drums.

                                        CUT TO:

AGENT SMITH and AGENT WHITE are killing everyone, and anything, in sight; Agents, Techs, Assistants, even The Janitor.

THEY, literally, KILL EVERYBODY in the DEA BUILDING...

                                        CUT TO:

INT. DEA BUILDING - MOMENTS LATER

AGENT ORANGE goes directly to the OFFICE of the DEA BOSS, killing 8 more people in the process.

ORANGE kicks the door in and rushes into the DEA BOSS'S OFFICE with his gun in-hand...

                                        CUT TO:

INT. DEA BOSS'S OFFICE - CONTINUOUS

                         DEA BOSS
                    (shocked by who he
                     sees)
                 AGENT ORANGE.

                    AGENT ORANGE
                    (facetiously)
          Yep, that's me, Sir. I got a
          bullet with your name on it...

AGENT ORANGE points his pistol at THE DEA BOSS and shoots
him directly in the forehead.

The DEA BOSS falls face-flat on his desk...

                                        CUT TO:

INT. DEA BUILDING - MOMENTS LATER

AGENT ORANGE, WHITE and SMITH have eradicated every AGENT
and every bit of personnel in the DEA BUILDING...

The THREE gather and observe the Hell they've allocated.

                    AGENT WHITE
          What now, Boss?

                    AGENT ORANGE
                 (snorts some coke)
          Get THE SHIT...

                    AGENT SMITH
          Yes, Sir!

                                        CUT TO:

INT. DEA BUILDING - MOMENTS LATER

SMITH and WHITE, each, walk out of the DEA BUILDING with
briefcases that are holding "THE SHIT".

"THE SHIT" is dope and cash.

                                        CUT TO:

AGENT ORANGE delays, and stays behind. He pulls pins out of
customized grenades, and rolls them on the floor...

The grenades are filled with the poison: 'AGENT ORANGE'. As
KIMBO ORANGE runs out of the DEA BUILDING the grenades
explode.

AGENT ORANGE walks out of the building, laughing like a
pure-Joker...

The virulent-ORANGE-chemical consumes the interior of The
DEA BUILDING and it covers the dozens of dead bodies that
are scattered throughout the BUILDING...

                              CUT TO:

EXT. DEA BUILDING - MOMENTS LATER

AGENT ORANGE, SMITH, and WHITE are met outside the DEA
BUILDING by the BLACK SUV in which they arrived in. The
AGENTS enter the BLACK SUV, and ORANGE'S DRIVER swerves off,
out of sight. The fatal orange-chemical slowly oozes out of
the DEA BUILDING...

The AGENTS are agents of CHAOS...

                              CUT TO:

                              4 YEARS LATER

INT. GROW-HOUSE - EVENING

                              YEAR: 2016

A bearded MAN, with long blonde hair, in his late 40's, is
in a GROW-HOUSE in WEWAHITCHKA, FLORIDA, in a very remote
location. There are no houses or people for miles, as it is
strictly private land. The MAN in the GROW-HOUSE is MICHAEL
TEDESCO.

In the GROW-HOUSE that MICHAEL is in are hundreds of some of
the dankest marijuana plants on Earth. The property, the
GROW-HOUSE, and the plants are owned by MICHAEL...

                              CUT TO:

He is walking through examining his plants, with his
Carolina-blue eyes. MICHAEL'S plants are in an infantile
vegetative-state; the plants are no where near ready to be
harvested.

MICHAEL has planted seeds for a new crop. He has 58 pounds
of pot prepared and packaged in his GROW-HOUSE, ready to be
sold and smoked...

                              CUT TO:

The GROW-HOUSE is close to MICHAEL'S CABIN. They are
adjacent to one another, and only separated by about 100
feet. However, MICHAEL'S GROW-HOUSE is much bigger than his
CABIN.

MICHAEL takes time to water the potting-soil he has placed the seeds in. Subsequently, he closely observes his marijuana-garden.

                    MICHAEL
               (amazed)
          Beautiful, just beautiful. This is
          better than I expected.

MICHAEL takes out a small wooden-pipe, and packs it with some pot. He then exits his GROW-HOUSE.

                              CUT TO:

EXT. WOODED AREA - MOMENTS LATER

The Sun is starting to set. It is a sight to behold for a battled-scarred man like MICHAEL...

MICHAEL pulls out a lighter and proceeds to hit his marijuana-filled wooden-pipe several times, hitting it as hard as he can...

It gets him higher than Hell.

                    MICHAEL
               (talking to
                himself jokingly)
          Mary-Jane, you've stolen my heart.
          Don't tell MARIA...

MICHAEL hits the pipe again. The pot is quite strong, as it is an experimental form of marijuana; an Indica-Sativa hybrid with a near perfect ratio of THC and CBD. He gets quite high off of the hits.

                    MICHAEL
               (facetiously
                talking to the
                pot)
          Damn, girl! You are mighty strong,
          I can't wait to harvest you. You
          have to be some of the best
          medicine I've tasted in a good
          while. You shall be known as:
          "Smack-Yo-Mama".

MICHAEL empties the pipe and puts it in his pocket. He then pulls out a pre-rolled from one of his jacket-pockets and lights it. He tokes the joint a few times. He then starts to

walk back to his CABIN through the WOODED AREA of his
property...

                              FADE TO BLACK:

                              CHAPTER TITLE
                              APPEARANCE:

II. YOU DON'T KNOW WHAT YOU GOT TILL IT'S GONE

                              FADE IN:

EXT. CABIN - MOMENTS LATER

MICHAEL finishes his joint, throws the roach down and stomps
it out as he walks. He is nearing his CABIN.

Having a FAMILY and a CABIN means the world to MICHAEL. He
is a very humble man...

He works for his family. He grows pot and he sells it. He is
a businessman. But first and foremost, MICHAEL is a
Family-Man...

He has worked all day. He has worked all week. He has worked
all his life...

As MICHAEL approaches the CABIN, he happens to notice a
secluded wild-rosebush in the WOODS to the side of the
CABIN. He has good eyes. All the roses of the bush are red
with the exception of one; there is a gorgeous black rose on
the bush. MICHAEL walks several yards into the WOODS to the
rosebush and grabs the black rose...

                    MICHAEL
          Hmm. I've never noticed this
          rosebush over here.
               (examining the
                black rose)
          MARIA will love this.

He puts the flower in one of his jacket-pockets and walks
out of the WOODS.

                              CUT TO:

After MICHAEL walks out of the WOODS, he stops for a moment
and admires his CABIN.

                    MICHAEL
             (soliloquy)
          Home-sweet-home.

He walks up the porch-stairs and enters his CABIN...

                                        CUT TO:

INT. CABIN - MOMENTS LATER

Inside the CABIN it is quite dark. MICHAEL goes to his
fridge and grabs some orange-juice; he drinks it right out
of the carton.

MICHAEL walks up the CABIN-stairs, chugging the OJ, and
enters his BATHROOM to take a shower.

                                        CUT TO:

                                        15 MINUTES LATER

INT. CABIN - LATER

MICHAEL exits the BATHROOM with a towel wrapped around his
waist; as he exits, a cloud of steam flows out from the
BATHROOM behind him; the steam is so heavy that it looks
like a ghost is following him.

                                        CUT TO:

MICHAEL is still drinking his orange-juice. He is shirtless,
and he has many battle-scars all over his back, chest, and
stomach; healed-up knife and gun-shot wounds...

MICHAEL walks down the hallway, with his jacket and
orange-juice in-hand, and enters his BEDROOM.

                                        CUT TO:

INT. BEDROOM - CONTINUOUS

MICHAEL cuts the lights on in the BEDROOM. He hangs his
jacket on the knob of the BEDROOM door. He finishes his
orange-juice and puts the carton on his dresser...

In the bed is his stunningly beautiful wife: MARIA TEDESCO.
She awakens as MICHAEL enters the BEDROOM...

                    MARIA
          Hey, Baby. I'm glad you're finally
          home. How is your crop coming
          along?

MICHAEL sits down on the bed at his wife's side...

                    MICHAEL
          It's going great, honey. I planted
          about a thousand more seeds
          today--it's a new breed I've been
          working on.

                    MARIA
          That's good, sweetie. I'm glad
          your garden is doing well and
          paying off.

                    MICHAEL
          Thanks, babe. How are the kids?

                    MARIA
               (smiling)
          MIKEY is doing great. He is at
          basketball practice. He has a good
          report card, all A's. APRIL is at
          a friend's house. She is doing
          fine. Her report card is all A's,
          too. She's been a little hostile
          here lately, but that's a 16 year
          old daughter for ya.

                    MICHAEL
               (smirking)
          She's at that stage, huh?

                    MARIA
          I reckon so.

     MICHAEL leans over his wife and kisses her.

                    MICHAEL
          And, how about you, my love? How
          was your day?

                    MARIA
          It went well. I can't complain.
          The restaurant was kind of busy,
          but that's better than it not
          being busy at all like last week.
          I made some decent money today;
          people gave me some pretty good
          tips.

                    MICHAEL
          Good, baby, I'm glad you had a
          good day. You know, I love you,
          right?

                        MARIA
            Yes, of course. You know that I
            love you more, right?

Both MICHAEL and MARIA smile at one another.

                        MICHAEL
                  (smiling)
            I don't know. I love you,
            astronomically. Exponentially.
            Infinitely. Unrelentingly.

                        MARIA
            The bigger the words, the more
            romantic you sound.

                        MICHAEL
            That reminds me. I have a surprise
            for you.

                        MARIA
            Really?

MICHAEL walks over to his jacket. He reaches inside of the
coat pocket, and pulls out something. He holds it in his
hands behind his back. He walks over to MARIA, and sits down
beside her.

                        MARIA
                  (excited)
            Let me see.

MICHAEL pulls the black rose from behind his back and hands
it to MARIA.

                        MARIA
                  (captivated)
            MICHAEL, it's absolutely
            beautiful.

MARIA gently places the black rose on the nightstand. Then,
she grabs MICHAEL wraps her legs around him and pulls him to
her.

                        MARIA
            Come here. Since we have the place
            to ourselves right now, take that
            towel off and give me some lovin,
            you romantic, you--

MICHAEL kisses MARIA and throws his towel to the side. He
and his wife begin making passionate love...

CUT TO:

INT. CABIN - MORNING

MICHAEL and his family; MICHAEL TEDESCO JR. or
little-'MIKEY', APRIL TEDESCO, and MARIA all wake up. All of
them are rising from their sleep. They congregate in the
kitchen...

                    MICHAEL
          How is everybody this morning?

                    MIKEY
          I'm all right, pop.

                    MICHAEL
          APRIL? MARIA? How are you two this
          morning?

                    MARIA
               (flirtaiously and
               smiling)
          I'm fine, sweety. But, I'm still
          tired from yesterday evening.

MARIA bumps MICHAEL with her hips. MICHAEL smiles at his
wife and kisses her on the cheek.

                    APRIL
               (yawning)
          I'm good, dad. How about you?

                    MICHAEL
          I can't complain, honey. I had
          long day at work yesterday, but I
          think it will be worthwhile. With
          this crop, we will be straight for
          a good while. I was thinking maybe
          we could take a family-vacation.

                    MARIA
          A vacation?--

                    APRIL
          --A vacation to where?--

                    MICHAEL
          --I don't know--where ever you
          guys want to go. I'm doing much
          better than I expected, and I
          would like to take you guys
          somewhere nice, somewhere
          overseas. I just need a change of
               (MORE)

                    MICHAEL (cont'd)
scenery.

                    MIKEY
            (uninterested in
            the current
            conversation)
What are we having for breakfast?

                    MARIA
I'm going to make some eggs,
bacon, and toast. Is that all
right with everyone?

                    MICHAEL
Sounds good to me, hun.

                    MIKEY
I want waffles.

                    MARIA
Well, I want a chocolate house but
you don't here me complaining. Do
you, son?

                    APRIL
            (texting on her
            cellphone)
A chocolate house? Whatever,
mom...

                    MIKEY
A chocolate house! That's sounds
cool! Can you really make a house
out of chocolate?

                    MICHAEL
            (pats MIKEY'S
            head, smiling)
No, son, she was just joking with
you.

                    MARIA
I'll fix you some waffles, baby.
How many would you like?

                    MIKEY
Four!

                    MARIA
            (to MIKEY)
You got it, buddy.
            (asking MICHAEL
            and APRIL)
                    (MORE)

                    MARIA (cont'd)
          You guys want waffles too, or
          what?

                    MICHAEL
          That's fine with me, honey.
          Whatever you want to fix, I'll
          take...

                    APRIL
          Same here, mom.

                    MARIA
          Okay, so waffles it is...

MICKEY exits the CABIN onto the front-porch.

                              CUT TO:

EXT. CABIN - MOMENTS LATER

MICHAEL sits down in his chair on the porch. As he sits down
he pulls out a baggy of marijuana, and a pack of JOB 1.5
rolling-papers. He proceeds to roll a joint. He rolls the
joint quite quickly. He lights it and begins smoking.

                    MICHAEL
                (soliloquy)
          There's nothing better than a good
          ol' fashion wake-n-bake.

MICHAEL continues smoking the joint, and as he smokes he
hears a noise far off in the distance. It is the sound of
three VEHICLES driving toward his CABIN...

                    MICHAEL
          What the hell?

MICHAEL puts the joint out. He gets up, and opens the door
to inquire with his wife about the incoming VEHICLES.

                    MICHAEL
          Honey?! Are you expecting anybody?

                    MARIA
          No, MICHAEL, why?!

                    MICHAEL
          I hear someone pulling up the
          road, that's all.

                         MARIA
                    (from inside the
                    CABIN)
               --Maybe it's the mail-man.--

                         MICHAEL
               --It's a little early, don't you
               think?--

                         MARIA
                    (from inside the
                    CABIN)
               --Yeah, but you know how sporadic
               the mail-man is. Sometimes he's
               here really late, sometimes he's
               early.--

                         MICHAEL
               --But I hear more than one
               VEHICLE, MARIA.

MICHAEL is suspicious of the incoming VEHICLES. He enters
the CABIN, and closes and locks the door behind him. He
immediately opens the window-blind to see who is pulling up
to his CABIN...

One ORANGE 1976 CORVETTE followed by two BLACK Federal
Agent-looking VEHICLES pull up in front of the CABIN...

The ORANGE 1976 CORVETTE is being driven by AGENT ORANGE.
The other two black VEHICLES are being driven by AGENT WHITE
and AGENT SMITH, respectively.

                                        CUT TO:

EXT. CABIN - MOMENTS LATER

The AGENTS exit their respective VEHICLES with
automatic-weapons in-hand.

AGENT ORANGE is wearing his signature Orange tie. SMITH and
WHITE are wearing solid-black ties...

                                        CUT TO:

The AGENTS start walking toward the CABIN, and immediately
unload their weapons on it. The AGENTS riddle the CABIN with
bullets with MICHAEL and his family still inside.

                                        CUT TO:

INT. CABIN - CONTINUOUS

MICHAEL ducks down to dodge the incoming gun-fire...

There's no cell-reception where MICHAEL lives. He cannot reach a phone anyway. Neither can his family, due to the heavy gun-fire raining in on the CABIN.

                    MARIA
          MICHAEL!!! What's happening?!

                    MICHAEL
               (yelling)
          MARIA! Get the kids to the
          basement!
               (in a dead panic)
          NOW!!!

MARIA, APRIL and MIKEY go down into the basement; there are no phones in the basement, so MARIA, APRIL, and MIKEY cannot call for help. MICHAEL is shocked by the appearance of The AGENTS. He has no weapons to defend himself or his family. All he has near him is a semi-automatic hunting rifle with a limited supply of bullets. MICHAEL grabs his rifle and readies it...

He has other weapons in the CABIN, but he is unable to reach them due to the flurry of bullets from the AGENTS...

Bullets are still flying through the CABIN. MICHAEL sits behind the kitchen counter, and prepares to retaliate against the AGENTS with what little firepower he has...

                                        CUT TO:

EXT. CABIN - MOMENTS LATER

The three AGENTS stop firing their weapons...

AGENT ORANGE inhales the gun-smoke from his rifle. He then snorts some cocaine, and subsequently exhales the gun-smoke...

                    AGENT ORANGE
          Slaughter is the best medicine.

                                        CUT TO:

The AGENTS reload their weapons and proceed to walk up the steps of the CABIN.

                                        CUT TO:

The AGENTS stand by the sides of the door...

                    AGENT ORANGE
                (yelling in a
                 manic tone)
          MICHAEL!!! Come out with your
          hands up!!! If you resist, you
          will die! If you don't resist, you
          will die!

                    AGENT WHITE
          We know your in there, MICHAEL! We
          also know your family is in there!
          We're going to kill them while you
          watch, you
          double-dealing-son-of-a-bitch!!!

                    AGENT SMITH
          Don't make it hard on yourself,
          MICHAEL! If you don't come out,
          we're coming in!

                                        CUT TO:

INT. CABIN - MOMENTS LATER

MICHAEL is in shock. He grips his rifle tight and prepares
for the AGENTS to enter the CABIN.

                    MICHAEL
                (talking to
                 himself)
          ORANGE? Oh, no...

                                        CUT TO:

EXT. CABIN - CONTINUOUS

                    AGENT ORANGE
          Are you ready, MICHAEL? Are you
          ready to die by my hands?! Ready
          or not, here I come!!!

AGENT ORANGE kicks open the front-door of the CABIN, and he,
SMITH, and WHITE tactically enter the CABIN...

                                        CUT TO:

INT. CABIN - MOMENTS LATER

As soon as the AGENTS enter the CABIN, MICHAEL rises up from
behind the kitchen-counter aiming his weapon at the invading
AGENTS. AGENT ORANGE shoots MICHAEL immediately after he
rises, and MICHAEL falls on the floor and loses hold of his
rifle...

                    MICHAEL
          AaHHH!!!

                    AGENT ORANGE
               (with great
                disdain)
          It's been 4 long years, MICHAEL.
          How ya been?
               (snorts coke)
          You piece of shit! You thought you
          could double-cross me, and get
          away with it?!
               (kicking MICHAEL)
          You thought you could just cut me
          off?! NO ONE SAYS NO TO ME!!!

                    MICHAEL
               (severely hurt)
          How did you find me, ORANGE?

AGENT ORANGE picks up MICHAEL'S rifle and throws it away
from him.

                    AGENT ORANGE
               (maniacal)
          Ah, you know people...they'll tell
          ya anything if ya hurt em just
          right. I located one of your
          buyers, and I knocked his teeth
          down his throat, broke his
          knee-caps, and slit his
          Achilles-tendons. He told me right
          where you'd be. I hurt the son of
          a bitch so bad that he was begging
          me to put a bullet in him. So, I
          put several in him. Now we're
          gonna hurt you and your family,
          just right...

                    MICHAEL
          Fuck you, you monstrous
          son-of-a-bitch...

                    AGENT ORANGE
Fuck me? No, no, no. Fuck you,
MICHAEL!
          (punches MICHAEL
           in the face
           several times)
We're gonna take your product.
We're gonna take your cash. You
owe me.
          (pacing back and
           forth)
And, I'm not a monster, MICHAEL.
You are The Monster. You were, you
are still, THE MAN IN BLACK...I
mean, hell, you terrorized the
terrorists in IRAQ and
AFGHANISTAN. You have over 150
confirmed kills under your belt;
all solo. You were the deadliest
man on the planet. Now, you're
just a family-man, huh? You've
gone soft, MICHAEL. But, you are
still a Monster: THE MAN IN BLACK.
You have a solid body-count.
However, it's no where near my
record of 416, soon to be 420.
See, you killed who your uppers
told you to kill. I killed my
uppers, and now I eradicate who I
want. That's the difference
between you and I. You're a
Monster; an immovable object. I'm
the unstoppable force of Nature
that moves men like you, MICHAEL.

                              CUT TO:

                    MICHAEL
ORANGE, you better kill me. If you
don't, I'm coming for you with all
I got.

                    AGENT ORANGE
          (laughing with
           insanity)
You got it, MICHAEL! But, before I
kill ya, let's have some fun.
          (punches MICHAEL
           repeatedly)
HA-HA-HA!

The three AGENTS continue to beat on MICHAEL. They are
beating the living-hell out of him...

                              CUT TO:

                         5 MINUTES LATER

INT. CABIN - MOMENTS LATER

MICHAEL'S face is bruised and beaten. He is lying on his
stomach on the floor of the CABIN. He is covered in his own
blood.

                              CUT TO:

AGENT ORANGE is standing over MICHAEL, pointing a 9mm-glock
at his head.

AGENT WHITE and AGENT SMITH have APRIL, MARIA, and MIKEY on
their knees, held at gun-point...

                    MARIA
          MICHAEL! Don't let them hurt our
          Children!!!--

                    MIKEY
          --Pop, please do something!

                    MICHAEL
          APRIL, MIKEY. It's all
          right--everything will be--

MICHAEL tries to get up.

ORANGE hits MICHAEL on the head with his gun...

                    MICHAEL
          -Ah!!!

                    APRIL
               (frantic)
          Daddy!!!

                    MARIA
               (trying to remain
                composed)
          --Everything is going to be
          fine.--

                    AGENT ORANGE
               (arrogantly)
          --MICHAEL, you know you had this
          coming. Look at you. You're
          bloodied. You're beaten. You're
          defeated. You're about to lose
          everything you've ever loved by my
                    (MORE)

                        AGENT ORANGE (cont'd)
           hands, and there is not a thing
           you can do about it.

                        MICHAEL
           ORANGE, you son of a bitch! Don't
           you dare hurt my family!!!

                        AGENT ORANGE
           You are in no position to tell us
           what to do or not to do. We are
           simply here to settle up. That's
           it. Death has found you and your
           family today, MICHAEL. I am merely
           a messenger of Death. We are in
           the right. You are in the wrong,
           and you know this. Now, it is time
           for you and your family to know
           Death...

AGENT ORANGE puts MICHAEL in a headlock...

DEATH is looming over MICHAEL and his family.

                        AGENT ORANGE
           Kill the Children, now...

AGENT SMITH and AGENT WHITE point their guns at the
Children's heads and shoot them while AGENT ORANGE forces
MICHAEL to watch...

MICHAEL'S Children die instantly...

                        MICHAEL
                   (shouting)
           NO!!! OH, GOD, NO!!!

MARIA starts sobbing with great agony...

                        MARIA
                   (sobbing)
           Not my babies!!!

AGENT ORANGE lets go of MICHAEL'S head...

WHITE and SMITH grab MICHAEL. They stand him up...

AGENT ORANGE stabs MICHAEL directly in his left abdomen...

MICHAEL doesn't even flinch; he grunts a bit, but he takes
the knife like it's nothing. ORANGE pulls the knife out of
MICHAEL'S abdomen after twisting and turning it...

AGENT ORANGE then walks over to MARIA...

                    MICHAEL
          I'm going to kill you! You hear
          me?! You three are dead-men!!!

                    AGENT ORANGE
          Not today, MICHAEL. Not today.

ORANGE grabs MARIA by the hair and tilts her head back...

                    MARIA
          --It's okay, MICHAEL. It's going
          to be okay.--

                    AGENT ORANGE
          --Experience Death.--

AGENT ORANGE, with his knife, slits MARIA'S throat like she
is cattle...

                    MICHAEL
          --MARIA!!!

MICHAEL nearly collapses but SMITH and WHITE hold him up...

AGENT ORANGE puts his blade in its sheath. He then takes his
9mm and points it at MICHAEL...

AGENT ORANGE shoots MICHAEL several times in the chest at
near point-blank range...

MICHAEL is seemingly dead.

                    AGENT ORANGE
          I'll get all the cash. You boys
          get as much of the product as you
          can, and put it in your rides.
          Search the property. Then burn the
          place. Burn everything.

                    AGENT SMITH
          You got it, boss.

AGENT SMITH and AGENT WHITE exit the CABIN and proceed to go
to MICHAEL'S GROW-HOUSE...

AGENT ORANGE stands still for a few seconds and admires his
works of Death.

                                        CUT TO:

INT. CABIN - MOMENTS LATER

AGENT ORANGE walks up to MARIA and MICHAEL'S BEDROOM. He
enters the BEDROOM.

                              CUT TO:

INT. BEDROOM - CONTINUOUS

AGENT ORANGE can smell money in the BEDROOM. He goes right
to the bed, and flips the mattress and box-spring. AGENT
ORANGE finds a satchel.

He looks inside the satchel, and it is full of 100 dollar
bills.

                    AGENT ORANGE
                  (soliloquy)
            For the Love of Money is the Root
            of all Evil. And, Goddamn, I Love
            Money.

AGENT ORANGE exits the BEDROOM with the satchel in-hand.

                              CUT TO:

EXT. CABIN - MOMENTS LATER

AGENT ORANGE exits the CABIN with the satchel full of
MICHAEL'S money; about $160,000. He places the satchel full
of cash in his ORANGE 1976 CORVETTE...

                              CUT TO:

While MICHAEL is lifeless, SMITH and WHITE are going through
his GROW-HOUSE; they seize the 58 pounds that MICHAEL had
prepared to sell.

AGENT SMITH and AGENT WHITE quickly stuff the dank-marijuana
into their VEHICLES...

                              CUT TO:

AGENT WHITE finds a large can of gasoline on MICHAEL'S
property. He pours gasoline all around the outside of the
CABIN...

                    AGENT ORANGE
            Burn his crop as well...

                              AGENT WHITE
               You got it, Boss.

                                             CUT TO:

WHITE pours the gasoline all over MICHAEL'S marijuana-garden
in the GROW-HOUSE...

He then pulls out a box of matches, strikes a match and
tosses the lit match on the gasoline-drenched garden,
setting the GROW-HOUSE ablaze...

                                             CUT TO:

Subsequently, WHITE walks up to the CABIN and lights it on
fire, with a match, with MICHAEL and his family still
inside...

                                             CUT TO:

The THREE AGENTS enter their respective VEHICLES, and take
off from the CABIN...

The CABIN catches fire very quickly.

                                             CUT TO:

INT. CABIN - MOMENTS LATER

MICHAEL lies on the floor of the CABIN, apparently dead. The
fire is spreading quite rapidly. The flames touch MICHAEL'S
arm...

MICHAEL rises up.

                              MICHAEL
                         (in great pain)
                    AaH!!!

MICHAEL gets up, and runs to the corpses of his family...

                              MICHAEL
                         (crying)
                    MARIA? APRIL? MIKEY? No-no. This
                    can't be. NO!!!

The fire is expanding. MICHAEL grabs his daughter and son,
and puts them on his shoulders.

                                             CUT TO:

EXT. CABIN - MOMENTS LATER

MICHAEL places his children outside on the ground.

He runs back into the burning CABIN to grab his wife.

                              CUT TO:

INT. CABIN - MOMENTS LATER

MICHAEL runs to his slain wife, and picks her up...

He runs outside with his wife's body right before the fire
starts to swallow up the CABIN.

                              CUT TO:

EXT. CABIN - MOMENTS LATER

MICHAEL places his wife beside his children...

He kneels by their bodies; he cradles his children and cries
a painful roar. He then puts their bodies down, and then he
grabs his wife and kisses her one last time...

                    MICHAEL
                 (sobbing)
            I'm so sorry! Please forgive me!
            Lord, please put their souls to
            rest!

MICHAEL gets up and limps into the WOODS...

                              CUT TO:

EXT. WOODS - MOMENTS LATER

MICHAEL limps along in the WOODS. He stumbles deep into the
WOODS. As he walks, blood drips on leaves.

MICHAEL reaches a trail and proceeds to limp down it.

As he goes down the trail, a WHITE RABBIT appears out of the
WOODS; it has blood red eyes. THE WHITE RABBIT hops along
down the trail; MICHAEL follows THE WHITE RABBIT. It takes
him to his SAFE-HOUSE.

MICHAEL walks upon his SAFE-HOUSE, which is very secluded,
and very deep in the WOODS...

                                        CUT TO:

EXT. SAFE-HOUSE - LATER

THE WHITE RABBIT is standing in front of the SAFE-HOUSE.
MICHAEL falls in front of the SAFE-HOUSE beside THE WHITE
RABBIT. He is losing consciousness. MICHAEL is able to pick
himself up and open his SAFE-HOUSE. When he opens it, THE
WHITE RABBIT disappears off into the WOODS. MICHAEL enters
his SAFE-HOUSE...

The SAFE-HOUSE is heavily fortified and very isolated...

                                        CUT TO:

INT. SAFE-HOUSE - CONTINUOUS

In the SAFE-HOUSE are weapons; various guns and blades.
Also, there is a very large stash of marijuana in the
SAFE-HOUSE, as MICHAEL is a pot-farmer. The stash is three
packaged pounds.

MICHAEL rips off his shirt and grabs a first-aid kit. He
fumbles the kit, dropping most of the stuff that's in it. He
is able to grab hydrogen-peroxide, bandages and
gauze-pads...he applies pressure to his gunshot wounds and
his knife wound; he is bleeding out quite severely...

                                        CUT TO:

MICHAEL goes to his marijuana-stash and breaks open one of
his pounds; there is a glass-pipe and an emergency-lighter
with the stash. He packs the pipe full of marijuana, lights
it and he hits it a few times as hard as he can. The pot
soothes his overwhelming pain. MICHAEL exhales and sits the
pipe down. He then falls down and passes out...

                                        CUT TO:

INT. SAFE-HOUSE - DAY

MICHAEL wakes up. He struggles to get up off of the floor,
but he manages to stand up.

                        MICHAEL
                    (talking to
                    himself)
                Oh, my God. My family is gone. Why
                am I still alive? How am I still
                alive?

MICHAEL grabs his pipe, packs it with more pot and smokes some more to ease his pain.

                    MICHAEL
          I-I-I can't do this.

He walks to a mirror in his SAFE-HOUSE, looking at himself.

                    MICHAEL
              (staring at
               himself in the
               mirror)
          You let them die! You did!

MICHAEL grabs one of his pistols and points it to his head while looking at himself in the mirror. He hears a female voice; it is MARIA'S voice.

                    MARIA'S VOICE
          Not yet, MICHAEL...

MICHAEL hears MARIA'S VOICE and continues to stare into the mirror with the gun at his temple. He begins to pull the trigger, but he stops and drops the gun. He starts crying in great anger.

MICHAEL punches the mirror, breaking it.

He stares into the broken mirror.

                    MICHAEL
              (greatly angered)
          I will avenge you, MARIA. I will
          avenge you, APRIL and MIKEY! I
          swear it! No matter what I have to
          do! I promise, with all my energy,
          I will find them and kill them. I
          will destroy them!!!

MICHAEL grabs a surgical-tool from his first-aid kit. He removes his blood-soaked bandages, and proceeds to remove the bullets one-by-one from his chest himself with the surgical-tool.

MICHAEL then sanitizes his wounds again, and places new gauze-pads and bandages on the wounds...

                                        CUT TO:

He walks up to his liquor-cabinet which has antique liquor in it. He breaks it open and he grabs the whiskey, pops the top, and chugs the liquor. Subsequently, he grabs his glass-pipe, packs it again and hits it a few more times.

                                        CUT TO:

MICHAEL sits down, and starts crying in anger. He chugs the
whiskey some more, hits the bowl again, and then throws the
whiskey on the floor, breaking the bottle. He gets up and
looks through his weapons.

His gun-rack is filled with many weapons, such as a 9MM
pistol, a G-18 pistol, two AR-15's, two M-16's, a
SPAS-12-gauge shotgun, and a Remington hunting-rifle. He
grabs the G-18 pistol, the 9MM, a M-16, and his
SPAS-12-gauge shotgun. MICHAEL then stumbles to his
ammunition-cabinet and grabs ammunition for the weapons he's
chosen. He then places the weapons and ammo on a table.

                                        CUT TO:

MICHAEL also goes to a closet within his SAFE-HOUSE. In it
are a bullet-proof vest, a black leather-jacket, black
military fatigues and boots, and a suitcase with a lot of
money in it; about 400 thousand dollars. The military
outfits that MICHAEL has in the closet are those he wore
while overseas doing assassination missions.

To the side of the closet are various medals; war medals.
There's even a picture of MICHAEL TEDESCO shaking hands with
The President...

MICHAEL was THE MAN IN BLACK. He served in IRAQ and
AFGHANISTAN.

MICHAEL pulls out his vest, black leather jacket, black
boots, black fatigues and places them on the same table as
the guns and ammunition; he also gathers some C-4 and Semtex
to go with his guns and ammo...

                                        CUT TO:

                        MICHAEL
                Those motherfuckers. I'll show
                them.

                                        FAST CUTS:

MICHAEL loads and readies his weapons. He suits up and puts
on his black fatigues, jacket, boots, and his bullet-proof
vest.

MICHAEL puts his weapons in a big duffel bag. He puts plenty
of pot in another duffel bag, along with plenty of cash.

Subsequently, he walks up to a CAR with a dust-cover on it.
He rips the cover off of the VEHICLE. It is a BLACK 1970
DODGE CHALLENGER...

After pulling the dust-cover off the VEHICLE, MICHAEL grabs
a pen and a notepad and writes down the names of the AGENTS
who attacked him; he knows who they are. They are his former
business partners: 1. RAY SMITH 2. CARL WHITE 3. KIMBO
ORANGE

Blood drips on the notepad as MICHAEL writes...

He rips the sheet of paper out of the notepad and puts the
list in his pocket. MICHAEL leaves the notepad in the
SAFEHOUSE...

                              CUT TO:

                              EXPOSITION:

As corrupt DEA AGENTS, ORANGE, WHITE, and SMITH extort
productive pot-farmers for cash and a big share of their
product and sell the pot to drug-cartels and various other
clients for massive profits...

MICHAEL was a primary supplier to the corrupt AGENTS for a
couple of years, but he discontinued their partnership
without notice and moved his family to WEWAHITCHKA from
MIAMI...

AGENT ORANGE doesn't allow those who work for him to quit.
AGENT ORANGE tracked MICHAEL down, killed his family,
attempted to assassinate him, and took his pot he had ready
to sell...

                              CUT TO:

EXT. SAFE-HOUSE - MOMENTS LATER

MICHAEL opens up his SAFE-HOUSE. The sun is shining bright
in the sky. MICHAEL packs his duffel bags holding his
weapons, pot and cash into his BLACK 1970 DODGE
CHALLENGER...

He gets into his CAR and drives it outside the SAFE-HOUSE...

MICHAEL'S CAR is a Great-Beast. It's a monster.

                              CUT TO:

EXT. SAFE-HOUSE - CONTINUOUS

MICHAEL has the lust for Revenge coursing through his veins...

                              FAST CUTS:

MICHAEL gets out of his CAR, closes his SAFE-HOUSE, gets back into his CAR and then takes off to find those who killed his family...

THE MAN IN BLACK IS BACK...

                              FADE TO BLACK:

                              CHAPTER TITLE
                              APPEARANCE:

III. HEAVY IS THE FIST

                              FADE IN:

INT. TORTURE CHAMBER - EVENING

ORANGE, WHITE, and SMITH have kidnapped a THIEF. THE THIEF stole some pot from one of ORANGE'S operations; he was a worker for ORANGE.

THE THIEF stole a half-pound of Pot from AGENT ORANGE.

THE THIEF is blind-folded and breathing heavily.

The THIEF is sitting in a metal chair...he tries to get up, but he is strapped down by metal straps that are restraining his legs, feet, arms and hands...

                    THE THIEF
          W-w-what the hell is going on?
          Where am I?! What the fuck?!

AGENT ORANGE lifts the blind-fold off of THE THIEF'S face.

                    AGENT ORANGE
          You, my friend, are in hell. You
          stole from me. Now, I'm going to
          steal your soul...
                    (snorts coke)
          ...You know, I got a joke for ya.
          You like jokes, kid?

                         THE THIEF
                     (shocked to see
                       AGENT ORANGE)
             N-no-Yeah!

                        AGENT ORANGE
             Okay. So, there was once a tribe
             of Indians in the far west. The
             Chief and his family lived
             comfortably there. One sunny day,
             the Chief's Son got curious as to
             how he and his siblings got their
             names, so, he began to question
             his Father. "Father, why do you
             call my brother: 'Black Crow'?".
             The Chief replied: "Well, Son,
             while your mother was giving birth
             to your brother, I walked outside
             of the Tee-pee, and I saw a Black
             Crow flying high in the sky...so,
             I named your brother: 'Black
             Crow'." "Wow!" responded the Son.
             "But, what about my sister? Why do
             you call her: 'Brown Bear'?" asked
             the naive child. The Chief
             replied: "Well, while your mother
             was giving birth to your sister, I
             walked outside of the Tee-pee, and
             I saw a Brown Bear walking about
             in the woods...so, I named your
             sister: 'Brown Bear'." "Wow!" said
             the Son. The Chief then said: "Why
             do you ask, 'Two-Dogs-Fucking'?".

THE THIEF lets out a fearful chuckle.

                         THE THIEF
             Ha.

AGENT ORANGE has a tall glass of ORANGE juice near him.

He picks it up and proceeds to chug it...

                        AGENT ORANGE
                    (finishes off his
                       ORANGE juice)
             Ah!

THE THIEF is trying as hard as he can to get out of the
metal chair. His attempts are an exercise in futility.

                         THE THIEF
             What the fuck?!

                         AGENT ORANGE
                       (pleasured by his
                         orange-juice)
              Damn! There's nothing better than
              FLORIDA orange-juice! Well, except
              Pussy, Weed, and Coke. But, other
              than that, FLORIDA orange-juice is
              the best thing there is.

                          THE THIEF
              A-a-are ya gonna kill me?!?!

                         AGENT ORANGE
                       (without even
                        thinking about it)
              Yep.

                          THE THIEF
                       (freaking out)
              Holy Fuck!

                         AGENT ORANGE
              Holy Fuck is right, my friend...

                                        CUT TO:

There is a device in the TORTURE CHAMBER along with a large
oven.

The device is similar to a Nebulizer, except it is
gargantuan, and the face mask is like-that of a helmet or
gas-mask. Also in the TORTURE CHAMBER there is a pound of
marijuana...

                         AGENT ORANGE
              Start it up, boys...

                         AGENT WHITE
              Yes, sir...

                         AGENT SMITH
              Yes, Sir...

AGENT WHITE grabs the POUND of marijuana.

He tosses it in the oven and allows it to burn.

                                        CUT TO:

The device takes all the smoke, THC, and everything in the
Pot and concentrates it in a contraption, basically a
man-sized bong close to the metal chair that THE THIEF is
restrained in...

The contraption is about 7 ft tall. It starts to fill up with tons of smoke...

AGENT SMITH straps the gas-mask onto THE THIEF'S face...

                    THE THIEF
                (screaming in fear)
            No, God! Please, no, God!!!

SMITH stands at a button near the oven. The mask is tight on THE THIEF'S face.

                    AGENT ORANGE
            Push the button, SMITH.

                    AGENT SMITH
            With pleasure, Boss!

SMITH pushes the button, and the smoke that is in the machine rushes into the tubes connected to the gas-mask.

THE THIEF takes in all of the reefer-smoke from the pound of pot, all at once. It severely suffocates him.

                                    CUT TO:

                    THE THIEF
                (coughing and
                 yelping)
            Aah!!! Aah!!!

THE THIEF is in shock, yet he is not dying. Life clings to him.

There so much reefer-smoke being absorbed into THE THIEF'S lungs that he starts having a seizure. THE THIEF is in pure pain as his entire body is being filled with too much pot-smoke...

                    AGENT ORANGE
            Just fucking die!

After standing and observing THE THIEF'S pain, AGENT ORANGE pulls his pistol and unloads the clip into THE THIEF.

                                    CUT TO:

THE THIEF quits shaking. He finally departs from life.

                                    CUT TO:

Heavy weed smoke gushes out of the gun-shot wounds of THE
THIEF...

AGENT ORANGE, AGENT SMITH, and AGENT WHITE laugh quite
maniacally, and all three AGENTS pull out joints, full of
MICHAEL'S pot, and proceed to smoke. They light their joints
and toke on them, and THE AGENTS continue laughing...

                                        CUT TO:

INT. AGENT ORANGE'S HQ - NIGHT

AGENT ORANGE'S HQ is a mansion right outside of MIAMI. It's
quite luxurious. The place is a hybridized work of
modernist-architecture and prairie-school design. However,
it was built on drugs and blood. All the walls of the place
are painted bright-ORANGE...

AGENT ORANGE is standing by a large fire-place, under a 100
Karat Gold-chandelier. Near him is a gilded-cage holding a
beautiful Crow.

                                        CUT TO:

AGENT ORANGE is talking with a CLIENT.

He is looking at a massive painting of a VIETNAM jungle
covered in the fatal-chemical: 'AGENT ORANGE'

AGENT ORANGE turns to face THE CLIENT...

                        AGENT ORANGE
                    (in mid-discussion)
                --Things have changed, for the
                worse, ever since BRODY got
                whacked and his brother got locked
                up...
                    (snorts coke)
                ...Business has been slow, going
                on 4 years now; things have been,
                let's say, patchy, an--

                        AGENT WHITE
                    (cuts off ORANGE)
                --Yeah, to say the least.--

                        AGENT ORANGE
                    (pissed by the
                     interruption)
                --WHITE, come on, man...don't cut
                me off, all right...
                    (snorts coke)
                ...Or I'll cut your fucking tongue
                        (MORE)

                    AGENT ORANGE (cont'd)
          out.

THE CLIENT sits back, and laughs at ORANGE and WHITE.

                    THE CLIENT
                 (patting his leg)
          HA-HA-HA!!!

                                        CUT TO:

ORANGE stands, prepared to lecture...

                    AGENT ORANGE
          Anyway, as I was saying--business
          has been stagnate, an--

AGENT WHITE is sitting across from THE CLIENT, at the same
table. ORANGE continues lecturing. WHITE is holding his gun
and has it lying on the table...

AGENT SMITH approaches WHITE from behind.

SMITH taps WHITE on the shoulder.

                    AGENT WHITE
                 (scared shitless)
          --Oh, shit!

WHITE'S gun spontaneously goes off and it blows THE CLIENT'S
head clean-off.

The Bullet passes through, and ricochets, and hits a GUY in
the background....

                    GUY
                 (very high pitched)
          Owwwwww!

                    AGENT ORANGE
                 (gives an apology
                  to the GUY)
          Sorry, GUY...
                 (pissed at WHITE)
          ...Jesus Christ, WHITE! You could
          fuck up a cup of water!

                    AGENT WHITE
          Sorry, Boss.

                    AGENT ORANGE
                 (snorts coke)
          If apologies from you were
          Nickels, I could buy a new BUGATTI
                 (MORE)

                         AGENT ORANGE (cont'd)
          by now, you ass-wipe...

SMITH and WHITE just stare at ORANGE, in a stupified daze.

                         AGENT ORANGE
                    (snorts coke)
          What the fuck, guys?! You gonna
          clean that shit up, or what?!

SMITH and WHITE rush about like a couple of imbeciles...

                         AGENT SMITH
          Yes, sir. Is it all right if I go
          home after we clean this mess
          up???

AGENT ORANGE pulls out a joint from one of his pockets. He
lights the joint and proceeds to smoke. The joint is filled
with MICHAEL'S pot...

                         AGENT ORANGE
                    (puffing the joint)
          Yeah, SMITH, of course. Do what
          you gotta do. But, WHITE, you stay
          in town and oversee the CLUB and
          do my deals while I'm gone.
                    (tokes the joint a
                     few more times)
          And, SMITH, I'll get in touch with
          you when I get back from Mexico.
                    (snorts coke while
                     smoking)
          ...I got business that I need to
          handle over there by myself. But,
          before anything, you two clean the
          brains and skull fragments up from
          off my shit...

                         AGENT SMITH
          You got it, sir.

                         AGENT WHITE
          Yes, boss.

AGENT ORANGE snorts more coke and continues blazing while
WHITE and SMITH clean up the bloody mess and the headless
dead body of THE CLIENT.

                                             CUT TO:

EXT. AGENT SMITH'S HOUSE - MORNING

MICHAEL is sitting in his CAR across from a HOUSE in a
random neighborhood; about 250 miles outside of MIAMI.
MICHAEL has been watching the place all morning.

The HOUSE is that of AGENT SMITH.

                              CUT TO:

MICHAEL exits the BLACK 1970 DODGE CHALLENGER and leaves his
weapons in it. He takes only a mysterious black fabric-kit
with him--he stashes the kit behind his back, under his
jacket.

MICHAEL walks up to the HOUSE and knocks at the door.

                              CUT TO:

INT. AGENT SMITH'S HOUSE - MOMENTS LATER

AGENT SMITH walks up the door, and opens it without asking
who it is, as he thinks it is his wife.

                              CUT TO:

EXT. AGENT SMITH'S HOUSE - CONTINUOUS

The door opens. MICHAEL and SMITH look at one another with
death-stares for a couple of seconds. SMITH immediately
tries to slam the door, and MICHAEL stops it with his foot
and busts open the door, making SMITH fall back. MICHAEL
enters the HOUSE, and slams the door behind him.

                              CUT TO:

INT. AGENT SMITH'S HOUSE - MOMENTS LATER

AGENT SMITH is shocked to see MICHAEL still alive. SMITH has
no weapon on him and starts backing away from MICHAEL...

MICHAEL walks towards SMITH.

                    AGENT SMITH
          You're supposed to be dead! How
          have you come back?!

                    MICHAEL
                (assertive and
                 angered)
          I'm back to give you absolute
                    (MORE)

                    MICHAEL (cont'd)
          pain.

                    AGENT SMITH
          Wait, MICHAEL...I-

                    MICHAEL
          -You are a dead man!

MICHAEL proceeds to beat SMITH with his fists. He punches
AGENT SMITH several times with great speed and power.

                              FAST CUTS:

MICHAEL then elbows, kicks, and punches SMITH relentlessly.
SMITH is being torn to shreds by the anger of MICHAEL. SMITH
punches MICHAEL, and MICHAEL takes the punches with ease.
His anger is unstoppable. SMITH tries kicking MICHAEL in the
head; MICHAEL catches SMITH'S leg and breaks it.
Subsequently, MICHAEL punches SMITH in the face, grabs him
by the neck, and choke-slams him through the living-room
table.

                              CUT TO:

MICHAEL is full of Rage and Power...

SMITH is an ant to a boot...

MICHAEL is the boot.

                    MICHAEL
               This is for my children, you
               son-of-a-bitch! This is for
               MARIA!!!

MICHAEL grabs SMITH, and jerks him up.

He proceeds to punch SMITH several more times with
unrelenting force...

MICHAEL savagely pounds SMITH in the face with his fists.

He brutally beats The AGENT to a bloody-pulp...

SMITH has been so severely beaten that he loses
consciousness.

                              CUT TO:

MICHAEL grabs SMITH and then proceeds to tie him to a chair
in the KITCHEN of the HOUSE.

                                        CUT TO:

INT. KITCHEN - MOMENTS LATER

AGENT SMITH awakens, tied to a chair. He has been beaten so
badly that his face is blue, black, purple, bloodied, and
unrecognizable. He can barely speak, but he is still
intelligible.

MICHAEL stands over SMITH.

                    MICHAEL
          You know, SMITH, I always thought
          you were the decent guy in
          ORANGE'S crew. But, you're just as
          sick as them. You helped murder my
          wife and children. You tried to
          murder me, and you failed. You
          burned down my home, you took my
          pot, burned my crop, and you
          destroyed everything I had. Now,
          it is your time to meet your
          demise; very slowly--very
          painfully.

SMITH is in great fear as he sees the hate, the anger, the
evil in MICHAEL'S eyes.

                    MICHAEL
          Now. You are going to tell me what
          I want to know while I mutilate
          you.

                    AGENT SMITH
               (spits at MICHAEL)
          I'm not telling you a Goddamn
          thing, MIKEY. Go ahead and kill
          me, I want to die!

                    MICHAEL
          I had a feeling you would say
          that...

                                        CUT TO:

MICHAEL pulls the black fabric-kit from behind his back, out
from under his jacket. He puts the kit on the
kitchen-counter and unfolds it. In it are neatly organized
scalpels, blades, scissors as well as a couple of small
hammers.

SMITH looks at the black torture-kit with great anxiety. He
tries to get out of the chair, but MICHAEL has him tied to
it too well.

                    AGENT SMITH
            I don't know nothing! I don't know
            a fucking thing, man! Untie me!
            Untie me, right now!!! You're
            making a huge mistake, man!!!
            You're the dead man!!! ORANGE will
            have an army after you!!!

                                    CUT TO:

MICHAEL fiddles with his torture-tools stroking them with
his fingers, ever so gently.

                    MICHAEL
            --You're right, RAY. I am a dead
            man. I'm a dead man walking. I
            honestly couldn't tell you how or
            why I survived what you fellas did
            to me, but I must be here for a
            reason.--

                                    CUT TO:

MICHAEL takes one of the small hammers and quickly smashes
SMITH in both of his knee caps with it.

                    AGENT SMITH
                (in agony)
            --AaHHH!!!--

                    MICHAEL
            --The reason being to right what
            you three wronged--to exact
            horrific vengeance in the name of
            glorious righteousness--that's why
            I am here with you today.

SMITH starts going into shock.

MICHAEL puts down the hammer. He takes a syringe from his
black fabric-kit. The shot is full of a customized
paralysis-agent. MICHAEL injects SMITH in the neck,
introducing the paralysis-agent to his blood-stream. Now,
SMITH cannot move his body whatsoever, yet he can still feel
pain.

                    MICHAEL
            Where is WHITE and where is
            ORANGE?!

                AGENT SMITH
          (in shock)
      I-I-I don't know. P-p-please,
      MIKEY, I don't know...

                MICHAEL
      So be it...

MICHAEL reaches for another tool in his kit. He gets a pair
of pliers.

                AGENT SMITH
      W-w-what are you doing?!

                        CUT TO:

MICHAEL takes the pliers, grabs a hold of SMITH'S right ear
and proceeds to yank it off with the pliers.

With in a few seconds, MICHAEL has ripped off a majority of
SMITH'S ear. SMITH cannot move, but he feels all the pain
being dealt to him by MICHAEL.

                AGENT SMITH
      Oh, GOD, no!!! Please, no!!!

MICHAEL puts the pliers down.

                MICHAEL
      God is not with you. He has
      nothing to do with this. Now, tell
      me what I need to know, SMITH.

                AGENT SMITH
          (in shock)
      O-o-okay, I'll tell you! WHITE is
      in MIAMI, at the CLUB, overseeing
      ORANGE'S business, b-b-because
      ORANGE is in MEXICO making a deal
      with the ESTEVEZ-CARTEL! There! I
      told you!

                MICHAEL
      See. That wasn't so hard, was it?

MICHAEL picks up a pair of surgical-scissors from out of the
kit.

                MICHAEL
      Now, you need not speak any
      longer.

MICHAEL takes the surgical-scissors, grabs SMITH by the head and cuts his tounge out with the scissors; blood starts gushing from SMITH'S mouth.

                    AGENT SMITH
          Ah...
               (coughing blood)
          Ah...

SMITH is bleeding out all over the KITCHEN floor.

MICHAEL puts the scissors down and then picks up his hammer again...

MICHAEL smashes SMITH'S arms, shoulders and collar-bone with the hammer. He then puts the hammer down and unties SMITH.

                    MICHAEL
          See, you're untied, now, go free.
          Do as you please, defend
          yourself...

                    AGENT SMITH
          Aah!!!

SMITH just sits in the chair as still as a statue. He cannot move at all because of the paralysis-agent that MICHAEL injected him with; however, AGENT SMITH can feel the retribution...

                    MICHAEL
          Well, I gave you your chance...

                    AGENT SMITH
          Aah!!!

MICHAEL grabs the hammer once more and slams it into SMITH'S face, denting his face in. SMITH falls out of the chair to the KITCHEN floor and dies.

                                        CUT TO:

MICHAEL puts his tools back into his black-kit and folds the kit back up. He then puts his jacket back on, grabs his kit, and proceeds to leave SMITH'S house.

                                        CUT TO:

EXT. AGENT SMITH'S HOUSE - CONTINUOUS

MICHAEL closes the door to AGENT SMITH'S house...

He checks his feet for blood. There is blood on his shoes. He wipes them on the welcome-mat; leaving blood on it. MICHAEL walks to his CAR.

He enters his BLACK 1970 DODGE CHALLENGER...

                                    CUT TO:

INT. BLACK 1970 DODGE CHALLENGER - MOMENTS LATER

MICHAEL sits in the CAR and takes a deep breath. He grabs his kill-list from his passenger-seat, grabs a pen, and crosses-out AGENT SMITH'S name on The List; his hands are shaking while doing so.

He reaches in the inside of his jacket-pocket and pulls out a picture of MARIA, APRIL, and little MIKEY. A single tear falls from MICHAEL'S eye. He kisses the picture, and then puts it back in his jacket-pocket...

He then grabs an already rolled joint, grabs his lighter, and lights the joint. MICHAEL starts puffing heavily on it. He takes several hits off the joint and holds in the smoke...

                                    CUT TO:

MICHAEL starts his CAR and then exhales a tremendous amount of smoke...

MICHAEL drives off, still blazing...

                                    CUT TO:

EXT. SMITH'S NEIGHBORHOOD - MOMENTS LATER

MICHAEL drives out of the neighborhood of AGENT SMITH.

                                    FADE TO BLACK:

                                    CHAPTER TITLE
                                    APPEARANCE:

IV. BRUTALITY IS BETTER THAN MORALITY

                                    FADE IN:

INT. DETECTIVE'S VEHICLE - DAY

A DETECTIVE by the name of JOHN MARSHALL is speeding through
the streets of MIAMI in his POLICE-CRUISER with his
police-siren screaming.

MARSHALL is a highly decorated officer of The Law. He is
white, and he is in his early 50's.

MARSHALL is a Serpico-type of detective; he's an honest cop
and a good man...

DETECTIVE JOHN MARSHALL seeks justice, not a paycheck. He is
incorruptible, experienced and uncompromising.

                    DISPATCH
               (through
                MARSHALL'S radio)
          All units, we have a 24-12 in
          progress on West 23rd...

MARSHALL snatches his radio.

                    DETECTIVE MARSHALL
               (talking into his
                radio)
          DISPATCH, this is MARSHALL. I am
          responding to the 24-12 and I'm in
          hot pursuit on West 23rd. I need
          back up, immediately.

                    DISPATCH
               (through
                MARSHALL'S radio)
          Back up is on the way, DETECTIVE.

MARSHALL puts his radio back in its holster, and pushes the
pedal to the metal...

                                             CUT TO:

DETECTIVE MARSHALL is in the middle of a pursuit. This is
MIAMI, FLORIDA...

MARSHALL is chasing down 3 ASSAILANTS. They've committed a
robbery, 2 murders, and they've also hit and injured an
innocent bystander, with their stolen VAN, in their reckless
getaway...

The ASSAILANTS have lost the squad-cars and the helicopter
that were chasing them. Now, MARSHALL is on their ass...

He's hell-bent on catching the ASSAILANTS...

53.

CUT TO:

EXT. ASSAILANT'S VAN - CONTINUOUS

The criminals: (ASSAILANT 1, ASSAILANT 2 and ASSAILANT 3)
are speeding recklessly through the streets...

CUT TO:

INT. ASSAILANT'S VAN - CONTINUOUS

The ASSAILANTS are wreaking havoc and they're not letting up
one bit...

They are armed with machine-guns and they are very high on
crystal-methamphetamine.

ASSAILANT 1 is driving, ASSAILANT 2 is in the passenger, and
ASSAILANT 3 is in the back. The ASSAILANTS are in a royal
blue hippie-VAN, of all things...

                    ASSAILANT 1
               (looks in rearview)
          What the fuck, man, we gotta cop
          behind us!!! Shoot that
          motherfucker!!!

                    ASSAILANT 2
          I got his tires...
               (looks at
               ASSAILANT 3)
          ...You shoot his windows!

ASSAILANT 2 and ASSAILANT 3, in a rage, break out windows of
the VAN and extend themselves outside of the windows. They
shoot at DETECTIVE MARSHALL'S VEHICLE...

                    ASSAILANT 3
               (letting bullets
               fly)
          Ah!!!!

                                        CUT TO:

EXT. MIAMI STREET - MOMENTS LATER

The ASSAILANTS relentlessly shoot at DETECTIVE MARSHALL; the
DETECTIVE is right on their tail...

Several bullets penetrate MARSHALL'S VEHICLE.

MARSHALL lays off a bit, trying to figure out a way to take the criminals out without causing civilian casualties.

                                        CUT TO:

DETECTIVE MARSHALL cuts quickly to the right of the VAN. Subsequently, MARSHALL rams his VEHICLE into the ASSAILANT'S VAN...

He can't knock them off the road.

He takes his pistol, extends it out of his window and shoots at the tire of the VAN, all while evading the ASSAILANT'S gun-fire. This happens very quickly. DETECTIVE MARSHALL hits the tire spot-on. ASSAILANT 1 fumbles the wheel, and the VAN goes tumbling and flips several times.

                                        CUT TO:

INT. DETECTIVE MARSHALL'S VEHICLE - MOMENTS LATER

MARSHALL stops his car. He grabs his radio once more.

                    DETECTIVE MARSHALL
               (talking into his
                radio)
          I need an ambulance. Suspects may
          be injured.

                    DISPATCH
          Paramedics have been dispatched,
          DETECTIVE.

DETECTIVE MARSHALL exits his VEHICLE with his pistol in-hand and proceeds to walk up to the VAN.

                                        CUT TO:

EXT. MIAMI STREET - CONTINUOUS

                    DETECTIVE MARSHALL
          Come out with your hands on your
          heads and your faces on the
          grounds, now!!!!

                    ASSAILANT 3
               (panicking)
          I-I-I can't feel my legs...

DETECTIVE MARSHALL cautiously looks inside the VAN.

None of the criminals had on their seat-belts. ASSAILANT 1, and ASSAILANT 2 are deceased. Their necks were broken in the crash.

ASSAILANT 3 has survived, but his neck is also broken, and he is seemingly paralyzed.

                              CUT TO:

DETECTIVE MARSHALL, standing by the VAN, sees that the ASSAILANTS are incapacitated. He puts his gun away and pulls out a cigarette. MARSHALL lights the cigarette, hits it hard a few times and exhales a lot of smoke.

                    DETECTIVE MARSHALL
                 (soliloquy)
          What a fucking day.

                              CUT TO:

Paramedics arrive, and they tend to the ASSAILANTS. Also, several POLICE OFFICERS start appearing at the scene in POLICE-CRUISERS.

DETECTIVE MARSHALL wanted to apprehend, not harm the suspects. He simply wanted to bring them in, and have justice deal with them.

He feels partly responsible for the deaths of the two ASSAILANTS, and the paralysis of the third ASSAILANT.

MARSHALL is a very ethical, moral, and respectable man. He puts the law first, and will not cross it. He goes beyond the call of duty, and does not see himself as a judge, but rather, he respects the justice system enough to catch criminals; DETECTIVE MARSHALL tries his best not to kill perpetrators...

Officers are all around. MARSHALL starts to go back to his VEHICLE. He feels his job is done...

He's regretful he had to hurt the suspects, but the suspects were stopped, and there were minimal civilian casualties; MARSHALL did what he had to do, and he did it well...

                              CUT TO:

INT. DETECTIVE MARSHALL'S VEHICLE - NIGHT

It is pouring rain. MARSHALL drives up to a LIQUOR STORE,
and exits his damaged VEHICLE.

                                        CUT TO:

EXT. LIQUOR STORE - MOMENTS LATER

DETECTIVE MARSHALL is smoking a cigarette. The rain drops
put out his cigarette. MARSHALL throws the wet cigarette on
the side-walk and enters the LIQUOR STORE...

                                        CUT TO:

INT. LIQUOR STORE - MOMENTS LATER

MARSHALL is a regular customer at this LIQUOR STORE...

He is an alcoholic.

He walks up to the counter, and the CASHIER already knows
what MARSHALL wants; he doesn't even have to tell him...

The CASHIER goes to the JACK DANIEL'S WHISKEY before
MARSHALL even speaks...

                    DETECTIVE MARSHALL
              5th of Jack, please...

                    LIQUOR STORE CASHIER
              Yes, sir, anything else for ya?

The LIQUOR STORE CASHIER simply asks MARSHALL if he wants
anything else simply as a formality.

                    DETECTIVE MARSHALL
              No, just the Jack for me...

The CASHIER rings up the alcohol and then bags it up. He
doesn't tell MARSHALL the price of the liquor because
MARSHALL already knows the price of it.

MARSHALL places four 20 dollar bills on the counter.
MARSHALL gets a fifth of JACK every other day and pays 80
bucks. The DETECTIVE likes tipping the clerks of the LIQUOR
STORE.

                    DETECTIVE MARSHALL
              Keep the change...

                    LIQUOR STORE CASHIER
                 (happily accepts
                  the tip)
            Yes, Sir. Have a goodnight.

                    DETECTIVE MARSHALL
            You as well....

MARSHALL exits the LIQUOR STORE.

                                        CUT TO:

EXT. LIQUOR STORE - MOMENTS LATER

MARSHALL gets into his VEHICLE, and slowly drives off from
the LIQUOR STORE. He's headed to his HOME. The rain starts
falling even harder...

IT RAINS ON THE JUST AND THE UNJUST ALIKE.

                                        CUT TO:

INT. MARSHALL'S HOME - LATER

MARSHALL opens his door, and enters his HOME. He takes off
his jacket and hangs it on his coat-rack. MARSHALL removes
his pistol with the holster and places them on the
kitchen-counter. He then takes his badge and places it with
his gun.

MARSHALL grabs a glass from his cabinet, fills it with ice
and pours himself a drink....

                                        CUT TO:

He sits at his office-desk, in his HOME, smoking a cigarette
and sipping his JACK DANIEL'S WHISKEY...

DETECTIVE MARSHALL is reviewing paper-work for cases and
looking over evidence. His desk is covered with paper-work.

                                        CUT TO:

INT. MARSHALL'S HOME - LATER

MARSHALL is passed out drunk at his office-desk.

He wakes up, and is still competent. He's more tired than he
is drunk.

He lifts his head up, and opens the desk-drawer. He pulls something out: a picture. The picture is of a woman and 2 children: MARSHALL'S wife, son, and daughter.

They were murdered in a car-jacking 5 years ago...

Whoever committed the murders was never found. The Case went Cold, much like MARSHALL'S heart. The DETECTIVE is filled with grief and sorrow. His Life has been made desolate by Loss...

Pain has nearly devoured his soul, yet he still seeks and serves Justice...

MARSHALL rubs his fingers on the picture of his family...

                    DETECTIVE MARSHALL
                  (sobbing)
          I miss you all so much--why can't
          you have justice? Why can't I be
          with you now?

Losing his wife and children led MARSHALL into alcoholism, yet, their deaths also strengthened his morality and honesty as a law-man...

                                        CUT TO:

INT. MARSHALL'S HOME - MOMENTS LATER

MARSHALL, still staring at the picture of his family, lays his head down. He passes out again...

                                        CUT TO:

INT. FLASHBACK SEQUENCE (FAST CUTS) - CONTINUOUS

He starts having flashbacks/visions of his family; he experiences Happy moments:

A woman, MARSHALL'S WIFE, smiling, saying: "I love you".

Two children playing in the yard, giggling with glee.

                                        CUT TO:

INT. MARSHALL'S HOME/DREAM SEQUENCE - CONTINUOUS

MARSHALL awakens with a great sadness...

He walks to the BATHROOM, and washes his face...

As he washes his face he closes his eyes.

MARSHALL opens his eyes, and suddenly blood is pouring out of the sink-faucet...

                                        CUT TO:

MARSHALL jumps back in horrific-awe of the blood flowing from the faucet...

                                        CUT TO:

MARSHALL is looking into the mirror; it begins to crack very slowly.

Suddenly, the mirror-glass breaks completely and exposes darkness...

Subsequently, blood splashes out of the mirror, from the darkness, all over MARSHALL. He turns around and yells...

                    DETECTIVE MARSHALL
                 (frightened by the
                  blood)
           Ah!!!

                                        CUT TO:

MARSHALL turns back around, and the mirror is fixed back the way it was. And, the blood is absent from his face and upper body.

He looks at his hands, and they are covered in blood.

MARSHALL hears the horrifying sound of his family screaming in pain...

He then hears a vile and demonic voice which ominously says: "...I'll get you too."

                                        CUT TO:

INT. MARSHALL'S HOME - MORNING

MARSHALL'S cell-phone is ringing. He shakes and stirs in an attempt to wake up from his Nightmare. All he can hear are the screams of his family...

He finally awakens at his office-desk. He is in a cold-sweat. MARSHALL answers his cell-phone.

                     DETECTIVE MARSHALL
              (talking into the
              phone)
        Y-y-yeah? This is MARSHALL.

We can't hear the voice talking to MARSHALL through the
phone, but the call seems rather important as MARSHALL
begins scrambling to get his things together...

                     DETECTIVE MARSHALL
              (into the phone)
        I'm on my way. I'll be there in
        30.

MARSHALL hangs up the phone and leaves his HOME in a
hurry...

                                  CUT TO:

INT. POLICE STATION - LATER

MARSHALL walks into the POLICE STATION. He walks directly to
the CHIEF'S OFFICE and knocks at the closed door...

                        CHIEF
              (from inside the
              OFFICE)
        Come on in, MARSHALL.

DETECTIVE MARSHALL enters the CHIEF'S OFFICE.

                                  CUT TO:

INT. CHIEF'S OFFICE - MOMENTS LATER

The CHIEF gestures for MARSHALL to have a seat...

MARSHALL takes a seat in the CHIEF'S OFFICE.

                     DETECTIVE MARSHALL
        How'd you know it was me, CHIEF?

                        CHIEF
        You're the only cop in the
        department that still has the
        common courtesy to knock--

A FEMALE COP bursts open the door of the CHIEF'S OFFICE
without knocking. She proceeds to just walk right in.

                         FEMALE COP
                    --CHIEF, I--

THE CHIEF points his finger at the intruding FEMALE COP.

                         CHIEF
                    --Not now, woman!

The FEMALE COP turns around, exits the OFFICE and shuts the
door.

THE CHIEF looks at MARSHALL...

                         CHIEF
                    See what I mean?

MARSHALL gets straight to business...

                         DETECTIVE MARSHALL
                    So what's going on, CHIEF?

                         CHIEF
                    Well, MARSHALL, we have a
                    situation in Northwest-FLORIDA;
                    WEWAHITCHKA, to be exact.

                         DETECTIVE MARSHALL
                    WEWA? What's the situation, sir?

                         CHIEF
                    Triple-homicide; two kids, and a
                    woman. I don't know all the
                    details, but I've been asked
                    personally by their police-force
                    to have you go up there and check
                    it out to see what you can find...

MARSHALL cringes at the notion of the woman and children
being murdered...The CHIEF is specifically speaking of
MICHAEL TEDESCO'S wife and children.

Without hesitation, MARSHALL accepts the request from the
WEWAHITCHKA police-department...

                         DETECTIVE MARSHALL
                         (without thinking
                          twice about it)
                    I'm on it, CHIEF...

                         CHIEF
                    You'll have to use your VEHICLE, I
                    know it's damaged, but I'll get
                    you a new one as soon as possible.
                    Just get to Wewa and help em out.
                         (MORE)

                         CHIEF (cont'd)
          Gather what you need, and go do
          what you do best, MARSHALL...

MARSHALL rises from the chair.

                    DETECTIVE MARSHALL
          Yes, sir.

DETECTIVE MARSHALL exits the CHIEF'S OFFICE. He is going to
WEWAHITCHKA, FLORIDA to investigate the triple-homicide...

                              CUT TO:

INT. MIAMI CLUB - DAY

A large group of MEN are lounging in a CLUB. It's a hangout
for ORANGE'S crew. WHITE is sitting in a booth, and some MEN
are standing guard, while others are simply drinking and
hanging out. Two BUSINESSMEN are sitting across from AGENT
WHITE.

                      AGENT WHITE
          We recently picked up a massive
          crop. It's the best bud around.

                     BUSINESS MAN 1
          We would like to collaborate with
          you on a deal.

                      AGENT WHITE
          Good.

                     BUSINESS MAN 2
          What is your proposal?

                      AGENT WHITE
          Well, considering the quality of
          the product, we're willing to do
          $1,200 per pound.

                     BUSINESS MAN 1
          I would like a sample to see what
          we're working with here.

                      AGENT WHITE
          Not a problem.

WHITE signals to one of his men to come to him.

                         AGENT WHITE
                      (to his
                       SUBSERVIENT)
                 Get me a nice sample, a couple of
                 nice fatties for the gentlemen...

The SUBSERVIENT goes into the back of the club to roll up
some joints for the BUSINESSMEN.

                         BUSINESS MAN 1
                 --Where is ORANGE?--

                         AGENT WHITE
                 --He's on a business trip, he'll
                 be back in a couple of days.--

                         BUSINESS MAN 2
                 --We just aren't used to dealing
                 with anyone but ORANGE. I'd feel
                 better if he were present.--

WHITE gets frustrated.

                         AGENT WHITE
                 --Look, I'm here. ORANGE is not.
                 I'm doing the deal for you guys;
                 take it or leave it.

BUSINESSMAN 1 whispers to BUSINESSMAN 2 for a couple of
seconds and then they turn to AGENT WHITE.

                         BUSINESS MAN 1
                 It's no problem. Let's do
                 business.

The SUBSERVIENT walks in from the back of the CLUB...

He provides the BUSINESSMEN with the rolled joints.

                         AGENT WHITE
                 Now, gentlemen, please, test our
                 product and share your thoughts.

Both BUSINESSMEN pull out lighters, and spark their
marijuana-cigarettes.

                         AGENT WHITE
                 This is not like our original
                 bud...this bud is a near-perfect
                 hybrid. It's a indica-Sativa, with
                 a flawless THC/CBD ratio.

The BUSINESSMEN puff on their joints quite hard. They immediately begin coughing.

>   AGENT WHITE
>   (being facetious)
>   Am I right? Or am I right?

The BUSINESSMEN finally quit coughing, and continue to hit the joint only a few more times. They both put out their joints in the ash-tray, refraining from getting too high. Obviously, just from the look on their faces, this is some really great pot.

The pot the BUSINESSMEN are smoking is MICHAEL'S weed.

>   BUSINESS MAN 1
>   We'll take 80 lbs. Can you do that
>   for us?

>   AGENT WHITE
>   Yes, we can do that.

>   BUSINESS MAN 2
>   Will it be convenient for you to
>   provide us with the shipment
>   tomorrow?

>   AGENT WHITE
>   (standing up with
>   his hand out)
>   Not a problem.

The BUSINESSMEN stand up and shake hands with WHITE.

>   BUSINESS MAN 2
>   You have yourself a deal. Give
>   ORANGE our regards.

>   AGENT WHITE
>   All right, fellas. I'll be in
>   touch with you tomorrow and we'll
>   complete the transaction.

The BUSINESSMEN nod their heads in approval. They proceed to exit the CLUB.

AGENT WHITE picks up his cell-phone and calls AGENT ORANGE.

>   AGENT ORANGE
>   (through the phone)
>   Hello?

                    AGENT WHITE
                (into the phone)
        We sealed it. They got 80.

                    AGENT ORANGE
                (talking through
                 the phone,
                 snorting coke)
        Good. Make sure you only give them
        5 pounds of TEDESCO'S batch. That
        shit is too good to sell. We'll
        sell em 5 of that and keep the
        remainder for us to smoke. Then
        we'll give them 75 of our KB.
        They'll be able to tell the
        difference in the other 75 pounds,
        but, if they try to retract on the
        deal we'll wipe em out.

                    AGENT WHITE
                (talking into the
                 phone)
        Yes, sir.

                                        CUT TO:

EXT. MEXICO HOTEL/BALCONY - CONTINUOUS

AGENT ORANGE is standing on a BALCONY at a HOTEL in MEXICO
CITY. He is smoking a fat joint full of the pot he stole
from MICHAEL...

                    AGENT ORANGE
                (talking to WHITE
                 on the phone)
        On another note, I've setup the
        arrangement with the
        ESTEVEZ-CARTEL; I'm giving them
        20,000 pounds of our mids, at $650
        per pound. I'll be back earlier
        than expected...
                (tokes the joint
                 hard several
                 times)
        ...I'll be in tonight. Get
        everything together. Prepare the
        trucks, the planes, the boats and
        the shipments, immediately.

                    AGENT WHITE
        You got it, boss, I'm on it.

ORANGE hangs up.

                                        CUT TO:

INT. MIAMI CLUB - CONTINUOUS

WHITE hangs up the phone.

He picks up the half-burned joints from the ash-tray that
the BUSINESSMEN left behind. WHITE puts one of the joints
behind his ear and he sparks the other...

                    AGENT WHITE
                 (coughs and talks
                  to the joint)
            You're almost too good to smoke,
            my dear...

                                        CUT TO:

EXT. MEXICO HOTEL/BALCONY - CONTINUOUS

A naked SPANISH BROAD walks onto the BALCONY to be with
AGENT ORANGE. She starts massaging his neck and shoulders.

                    SPANISH BROAD
            Everything all right, Papi?

                    AGENT ORANGE
            Shut up, bitch, I'm not your papi.
            Get your hands off of me. Get back
            in the room and get the fucking
            coke ready...

THE SPANISH BROAD rolls her eyes and proceeds to go back
inside.

ORANGE tokes his joint and gets up from his seat. He then
tosses his joint off the BALCONY, walks into the HOTEL room
and slams the glass sliding-door behind him.

                                        CUT TO:

INT. BLACK 1970 DODGE CHALLENGER - CONTINUOUS

MICHAEL is cruising in his BLACK 1970 DODGE CHALLENGER...

He is headed to MIAMI. He is riding, smoking a joint, and
listening to Mozart: 'The Clarinet Concerto Adagio'

                                        CUT TO:

MICHAEL starts to enter a trance while smoking. He has
visions of his children, his wife, and his life before their
deaths. He hits the joint really hard. Subsequently, a tear
falls from his right eye. He pushes the pedal harder, nearly
flooring it...

MICHAEL is ready to complete his revenge. He is going after
ORANGE, WHITE, and whoever is with them.

MICHAEL is in great pain. His pain is, ironically enough,
his greatest strength.

He is driving his Beast of a CAR, with great aggression and
laser-focus; moving as fast as he can to get the men who
took everything from him...

He is thinking only about avenging his family.

                                        CUT TO:

EXT. CABIN/MURDER-SCENE - DAY

This is the MURDER-SCENE where MICHAEL'S family was slain.

There are fire-fighter crews just finishing putting out the
flames of the burned CABIN and GROW-HOUSE.

There are forensic-investigator teams, local law-enforcement
officers, DEA Agents, and even F.B.I Agents at the scene;
some are taking photos, some are collecting pieces of
evidence, and others are just standing around in awe of the
mayhem...

                                        CUT TO:

INT. DETECTIVE MARSHALL'S VEHICLE - CONTINUOUS

DETECTIVE MARSHALL is driving up to the MURDER-SCENE...

He is listening to music: JOHNNY CASH'S Live performance at
Folsom Prison...

MARSHALL is a lawman of ethics, and of strict moral-code.
He's been assigned to the case in WEWAHITCHKA, out of MIAMI,
because he's one of the best detectives in all of the state
of FLORIDA, and the WEWAHITCHKA police are specifically
seeking his help...

The DETECTIVE parks and exits his VEHICLE.

CUT TO:

EXT. CABIN/MURDER-SCENE - MOMENTS LATER

MARSHALL walks around and closely observes the area. There are countless shell-casings lying around. The GROW-HOUSE and the CABIN are completely burned. MARSHALL sees the spot where MICHAEL'S deceased wife and kids were laying, as there are bloodstains on the ground. The MURDER-SCENE disturbs MARSHALL deeply...

                    DETECTIVE MARSHALL
               (talking to
                himself, in awe
                of the
                murder-scene)
          Damn, and I thought I'd seen it
          all. Sweet baby-Jesus on the
          cross...

A POLICE OFFICER walks up to DETECTIVE MARSHALL...

                    OFFICER DUDLEY
          DETECTIVE?

                    DETECTIVE MARSHALL
          Yes, I'm DETECTIVE MARSHALL. And
          you are?--

                    OFFICER DUDLEY
          --OFFICER DUDLEY, Sir. We've been
          expecting you.

                    DETECTIVE MARSHALL
          Brief me, DUDLEY, what do we got?

                    OFFICER DUDLEY
          Well, sir, we've concluded this is
          a homicide. We know that the
          children were murdered by
          gun-shots and the woman had her
          throat slit. The CABIN, and the
          GROWHOUSE were burned down as a
          result of arson; oddly enough, a
          MICHAEL TEDESCO lived here as
          well. We assume that this was
          possibly a three-to-four man job.
          We haven't found TEDESCO'S body
          yet, and we aren't sure if he was
          or was not involved in the
          incident. Also, we found a lot of
          burned marijuana plants. He must
          have been a pot-farmer. But, other
                    (MORE)

                         OFFICER DUDLEY (cont'd)
          than that, really we have no
          motive or any suspects other than
          TEDESCO, so I've been told. He
          could have been a conspirator in
          the crime. We gathered some
          sufficient evidence, but we really
          don't have any solid leads.

                         DETECTIVE MARSHALL
          Have you done a thorough search of
          the grounds for TEDESCO?

                         OFFICER DUDLEY
          Yes, sir, very thorough. We still
          have no idea where this fella
          could be.

                         DETECTIVE MARSHALL
                    (with authority)
          Well, I want you to look out there
          again. If this man was here when
          this happened; he either did it,
          or he was also a victim. I want to
          know why he's not here. I want you
          to find his hideout in those
          woods; I know in my gut he has one
          out there somewhere, and we need
          to find it.

                         OFFICER DUDLEY
          I'm on it.

It disgusts MARSHALL to know that a woman and two children
were murdered. It makes his blood boil.

MARSHALL notices tire tracks...

He walks along the tire tracks, examining them; he notices
that 3 VEHICLES were on the property. He also sees
foot-prints. He sees that there are at least three sets of
foot prints.

                         DETECTIVE MARSHALL
                    (soliloquy)
          TEDESCO didn't do it, that's for
          sure. This was a three man job.
          This was a premeditated attack.

DUDLEY comes running toward MARSHALL...

                         OFFICER DUDLEY
                      (yelling from afar)
          They found it, sir, the hideout! I
          just got the message on the radio!

                       DETECTIVE MARSHALL
                      (rushing, running
                        to his CAR)
          Come on, I'll drive us. You can
          help me examine the place, DUDLEY.

                         OFFICER DUDLEY
                      (excited and
                       running to
                       MARSHALL'S CAR)
          Yes, sir!

MARSHALL and DUDLEY hastily get into MARSHALL'S VEHICLE, and
the two proceed to MICHAEL'S SAFE-HOUSE in the WOODS.

                                        CUT TO:

EXT. THE WOODS - CONTINUOUS

MARSHALL and DUDLEY travel down a tortuous trail that leads
to MICHAEL'S SAFE-HOUSE...

                                        CUT TO:

EXT. SAFE-HOUSE - MOMENTS LATER

MARSHALL and DUDLEY arrive at the SAFE-HOUSE...

They hop out of the VEHICLE, and cautiously enter the
SAFE-HOUSE...

There are cop cars, forensic vans, and other vehicles parked
outside of the SAFE-HOUSE...

                                        CUT TO:

INT. SAFE-HOUSE - CONTINUOUS

There is a forensic team in the SAFE-HOUSE...

MARSHALL is displeased; he wants to inspect the building
himself.

                                        CUT TO:

                    DETECTIVE MARSHALL
                 (with authority)
          All right, guys, get out of here.

The FORENSIC INVESTIGATORS look at MARSHALL and just stare.

                    DETECTIVE MARSHALL
          Allow me to repeat with some
          clarification: GET THE FUCK OUT OF
          HERE, RIGHT NOW!

                    FORENSIC INVESTIGATOR
                 (scrambling about)
          You heard the man, people! Let's
          move out!

The FORENSIC INVESTIGATORS scramble around, and they
practically run out of the SAFEHOUSE...

                    FORENSIC INVESTIGATOR
          DUDLEY, come on!

                    OFFICER DUDLEY
          Nah...
                 (points at
                 MARSHALL with his
                 thumb)
          ...I'm with him.

MARSHALL now has the SAFE-HOUSE to himself. He allows DUDLEY
to stay in the SAFE-HOUSE while he inspects.

DETECTIVE MARSHALL and OFFICER DUDLEY are in awe of what
they see in the SAFE-HOUSE...

                    DETECTIVE MARSHALL
          Damn. This is a small fortress.
          Who the hell is this guy?

MARSHALL puts on a pair of black inspection-gloves and
begins snooping, trying to see where MICHAEL may have
disappeared to.

DETECTIVE MARSHALL observes MICHAEL'S ammo and gun
storage...he also sees a couple of pictures of MICHAEL'S war
days and the picture of MICHAEL shaking hands with the
president...

DUDLEY looks over MARSHALL'S shoulder, following his lead...

                    OFFICER DUDLEY
          So, this guy is a veteran?

                    DETECTIVE MARSHALL
          It appears so. From what I can
          tell, this guy was high up in the
          service. It seems that he was
          Ranger Battalion. Look at these
          medals, and these weapons. He was
          probably an operative or a
          spec-ops trainer, maybe both.
          Yeah. We're not dealing with your
          average fellow. This guy is the
          real deal...

                    OFFICER DUDLEY
          Why would a military man get into
          the marijuana business?

                    DETECTIVE MARSHALL
          That's a good question, DUDLEY...

MARSHALL walks around examining the entirety of the
SAFE-HOUSE. He sees the blood, and the mess that MICHAEL
left behind and it makes him quite curious.

MARSHALL, out of all the clues in the room, finds the
notepad that MICHAEL used to write down the Renegade AGENT'S
names.

MARSHALL notices the blood on the notepad, and knows it
means something...

                    DETECTIVE MARSHALL
          DUDLEY, you gotta pencil?

DUDLEY pats his pockets down and finds a pencil.

                    OFFICER DUDLEY
          Yeah, sure, here you go, sir.

                    DETECTIVE MARSHALL
              (takes the pencil
               from DUDLEY)
          Thanks.

MARSHALL then uses the pencil, and scribbles over the
indents made by MICHAEL, when he pressed down on the notepad
to write those names. Luckily, the pencil reveals MICHAEL'S
List to MARSHALL: 1. RAY SMITH 2. CARL WHITE 3. KIMBO
ORANGE...

                                        CUT TO:

MARSHALL examines The List...

                    DETECTIVE MARSHALL
          Interesting...

DETECTIVE MARSHALL takes off his gloves and stuffs them into
his coat-pocket. MARSHALL then pulls out a cigarette, and
lights it up; cigarettes help him think and theorize.

                    OFFICER DUDLEY
          What is it, sir?

                    DETECTIVE MARSHALL
                (puffing his
                 cigarette)
          Ah, it's nothing, just a little
          clue. But nothing substantive.
          Anyway, it seems TEDESCO was
          pretty badly injured. It looks
          like he came directly here from
          the CABIN, fixed himself up,
          grabbed some things, grabbed his
          CAR and took off...I wonder where
          to?

MARSHALL thinks deeply to himself...his gut instinct kicks
in. He knows where MICHAEL is headed: MIAMI. DETECTIVE
MARSHALL knows that MICHAEL is headed to get the untouchable
AGENT: KIMBO ORANGE

                    DETECTIVE MARSHALL
                (throws his
                 cigarette down
                 and stomps it out)
          Well, shit in my soup and call it
          beef-stew. You ever been exposed
          to AGENT ORANGE, kid?

                    OFFICER DUDLEY
          The chemical? Well, no.

                    DETECTIVE MARSHALL
          No, not the chemical. I'm talking
          about The Man.

                    OFFICER DUDLEY
          I thought that guy was a myth?

                    DETECTIVE MARSHALL
          He's real. And he is the most evil
          son-of-a-bitch on this planet.
          AGENT ORANGE is more dangerous
          than the chemical itself.

                    OFFICER DUDLEY
          What's he got to do with this,
          DETECTIVE?

                    DETECTIVE MARSHALL
          I gotta go. TEDESCO is headed to
          MIAMI. I'll drop you off with your
          people. This is gonna be worse
          than I thought...

DETECTIVE MARSHALL proceeds to rush out of the SAFE-HOUSE.
DUDLEY follows his lead.

                              CUT TO:

INT. DETECTIVE MARSHALL'S VEHICLE - MOMENTS LATER

MARSHALL is zooming in his CAR...

He pulls out his cell-phone to call the CHIEF...

                    CHIEF
              (through the phone)
          Hello?

                    DETECTIVE MARSHALL
          CHIEF, I'm on my way back. We have
          a situation on our hands.

                    CHIEF
              (through the phone)
          You're already headed back? What
          do ya mean, MARSHALL? What kind of
          situation?

                    DETECTIVE MARSHALL
          Sir, just get everybody ready and
          mobilized. All Hell's about to
          break loose in MIAMI...

                              CUT TO:

EXT. BLACK 1970 DODGE CHALLENGER - CONTINUOUS

MICHAEL passes a sign that reads: "Welcome to Miami". He is
moving like a bat out of Hell.

                              CUT TO:

EXT. PHARMACY - MOMENTS LATER

MICHAEL arrives at a PHARMACY to get first-aid supplies as
his wounds are worsening, and his supplies are depleting.

He takes off his bullet proof vest, and slowly pulls up his
shirt. His bandages are covered in blood, and he is still
bleeding out. MICHAEL'S wounds are quite severe.

He goes into the PHARMACY, not caring how militant he looks.

                              CUT TO:

INT. PHARMACY - MOMENTS LATER

MICHAEL scopes the aisles. He grabs hydrogen peroxide,
gauze, tweezers, tape, and many other first-aid supplies. He
is bleeding on the floor of the PHARMACY...

After getting the supplies, MICHAEL goes to the counter of
the PHARMACY to pay the CASHIER...

                    CASHIER
          Will that be all for you, sir?

                    MICHAEL
          Yes...

                    CASHIER
          That'll be 38.46, sir.

MICHAEL gives the man two twenties and rushes out of the
PHARMACY.

                    CASHIER
          Sir, your change!

                    MICHAEL
               (in severe pain)
          Fuck the change!

MICHAEL stumbles out of the PHARMACY.

                              CUT TO:

EXT. PHARMACY - CONTINUOUS

MICHAEL moves quickly to his CAR, blood is pouring onto the
concrete of the parking-lot. As he walks to his CAR he
almost collapses. He is loosing blood and consciousness.

He fights through the pain and gets in the BLACK 1970 DODGE CHALLENGER with the first-aid supplies. MICHAEL starts his CAR and takes off from the PHARMACY.

                                        CUT TO:

EXT. MOTEL - DAY

MICHAEL pulls into the parking-lot of a random MOTEL. He gets out of the CAR, as he plans on getting a ROOM. His injuries and wounds are worsening by the second.

                                        CUT TO:

INT. MOTEL LOBBY - MOMENTS LATER

A RECEPTIONIST is standing at the front-desk of the MOTEL LOBBY. She is reading a magazine. She ignores MICHAEL'S entrance.

MICHAEL puts his hands on the counter. He has blood on his hands and this gets the RECEPTIONIST'S attention.

                    RECEPTIONIST
                (fearfully)
          How may I help you, sir?

                    MICHAEL
          I need a room.

                    RECEPTIONIST
          W-w-well, we have many rooms
          available. Would you like a
          single? A double? You may choose
          your room, sir.

                    MICHAEL
                (in tremendous
                 pain)
          All right, thank you. I'll take
          any room...

                    RECEPTIONIST
          Not a problem. You can have ROOM
          45. How many nights would you like
          the ROOM?

                         MICHAEL
                    (in great pain)
               Four. It doesn't matter, just
               however many....

                         RECEPTIONIST
               That'll be 135.67, sir.

                                        CUT TO:

MICHAEL reaches for his wallet and he struggles doing so.

                         RECEPTIONIST
               Are you all right, sir?

                         MICHAEL
               I'll make it...

MICHAEL pulls out his wallet and hands the RECEPTIONIST two
100 hundred dollar bills. She looks at the money quite
bewildered, as there is blood on it...

                         RECEPTIONIST
               But, sir, its only 1-

MICHAEL interrupts her.

                         MICHAEL
               -I don't care, keep the change...

                         RECEPTIONIST
               All right, here's your key, sir.

The RECEPTIONIST grabs the key and hands it to MICHAEL.
MICHAEL snatches the key and limps out of the MOTEL LOBBY.

                                        CUT TO:

EXT. MOTEL - MOMENTS LATER

MICHAEL goes to his CAR, grabs his medical supplies and he
grabs his two large duffel bags.

He then walks to the door of ROOM 45...

MICHAEL quickly unlocks the door.

He enters the ROOM...

                                        CUT TO:

INT. ROOM 45 - CONTINUOUS

MICHAEL shuts the door with his foot and drops his bags.

                                        CUT TO:

INT. ROOM 45 - MOMENTS LATER

MICHAEL takes his medical supplies and enters the bathroom.
He takes off his vest, fatigues, boots, and bandages.

He then takes a shower.

                                        CUT TO:

MICHAEL is bleeding out quite heavily...

His blood mixes with the water, and the mixture swirls down
the drain...

                                        CUT TO:

Having exited the shower, MICHAEL has a towel around his
waist. He examines his wounds in the mirror.

He then takes his medical supplies and begins doctoring
himself.

MICHAEL pours hydrogen peroxide on his wounds, and wraps
them in gauze and bandages.

                                        CUT TO:

INT. ROOM 45 - EVENING

MICHAEL changes back into his all-black uniform and puts on
his black leather-jacket.

                                        CUT TO:

MICHAEL grabs both his duffel bags. He then takes some pot
and some joint papers out of one bag. He rolls several fat
joints, grabs his lighter and proceeds to smoke one of his
joints to ease his body pain from his wounds.

                    MICHAEL
               (hits the joint a
                few times)
          That's better...

He hits the joint a few more times, and then puts it out. He then takes his gun-bag, with the weapons and ammo in it, and he pulls out his G-18, his M-16, and his SPAS-12-gauge shotgun. He readies the weapons and then puts them back into the bag.

MICHAEL stashes his duffel bag, with the weed and money in it, in the ceiling of the room; he does not expect to get it back.

MICHAEL then grabs his pre-rolled joints, grabs his weapons bag, and proceeds to exit the ROOM 45.

                              CUT TO:

EXT. MOTEL - MOMENTS LATER

MICHAEL places his weapons in his CAR, gets inside and sparks his unfinished joint. He cranks up the CAR and then cranks up the Mozart music.

MICHAEL leaves the MOTEL; fast and furious...

                              FADE TO BLACK:

                              CHAPTER TITLE
                              APPEARANCE:

V. DEATH ALWAYS COMES TOO EARLY OR TOO LATE

                              FADE IN:

INT. MIAMI CLUB - EVENING

WHITE is having a drink simply hanging out at ORANGE'S CLUB. The TV is on and it happens to be on the news.

                              CUT TO:

                     NEWS REPORTER
                  (on TV)
             Earlier this week authorities
             stumbled across a gruesome scene.
             The bodies of two children, and a
             middle-aged woman were found
             outside of a remote CABIN in
             WEWAHITCHKA, FLORIDA. They were
             brutally murdered; the children by
             gun, the woman by knife...
                  (clears throat)
             ...the residence at which the
             bodies were found was burned down.
                  (MORE)

                         NEWS REPORTER (cont'd)
The fire is suspected to have been
caused by arson. The property is
believed to have been partially
used as a marijuana farm, although
no marijuana was found or seized;
it appears that most all of it was
burned, along with a GROW-HOUSE
that was on the property near the
CABIN. The victims: MARIA TEDESCO,
MICHAEL TEDESCO JR., and APRIL
TEDSCO, were viciously attacked by
at least three assailants,
according to authorities. Police
are puzzled by the fact that the
father and husband of the
respective victims, MICHAEL
TEDESCO, was not found, but they
believe he may have been involved
with in incident and that he is
still alive. Authorities suspect
he is the owner of the
marijuana-farm that is on the
property. The police also found a
SAFE-HOUSE further off the
property in the woods. It has been
verified that it is a part of the
TEDESCO property, and has been
suggested that MICHAEL TEDESCO may
have went there sometime after the
murders. If you have any
information concerning this
incident or any information on the
whereabouts of MICHAEL TEDESCO,
seen here...
          (MICHAEL'S picture
           appears on the
           screen)
...call the WEWAHITCHKA police
immediately.

                                   CUT TO:

WHITE stands up out of his chair in shock, and spits alcohol
from his mouth.

AGENT WHITE drops his drink on the floor, and the glass
breaks.

                    AGENT WHITE
                (talking to
                himself)
          Holy-Shit!!! The son-of-a-bitch is
          still alive!

WHITE quickly reaches for his phone and immediately calls
AGENT ORANGE. AGENT WHITE is in a dead-panic...

ORANGE picks up the phone.

                    AGENT ORANGE
                (voice through the
                phone)
          What is it now, CARL?

                    AGENT WHITE
          Boss, we have a serious problem...

                                        CUT TO:

INT. CAR - CONTINUOUS

ORANGE is being driven around MEXICO CITY. He's talking to
WHITE on the phone...

                    AGENT ORANGE
                (talking to WHITE
                on the phone)
          What the hell's wrong?!

                                        CUT TO:

EXT. MIAMI CLUB - CONTINUOUS

WHITE walks outside of the CLUB scared to Death...

WHITE rubs his hand through his hair quite nervously.

                    AGENT WHITE
                (talking into the
                phone to ORANGE)
          He's still alive!

                    AGENT ORANGE
                (confused)
          Who? What do you mean, CARL?

                    AGENT WHITE
          MICHAEL! He's still breathing,
          KIMBO!!!

                    AGENT ORANGE
          What?!

An engine can be heard roaring off in the distance...

A GOON walks outside to see what the noise is. AGENT WHITE
is ignoring it as he is talking to AGENT ORANGE. The noise
is very distant, but also very distinct.

                    AGENT WHITE
          I just saw it on the fucking news!
          They said he's still alive!

                    GOON
          Boss?

                    AGENT WHITE
          Can't you see I'm talking on the
          fucking phone, you imbecile!!!

                    AGENT ORANGE
                 (through the phone
                  to WHITE)
          Make him dead!

                    GOON
          Boss, who is that heading toward
          us?

WHITE looks down the road. He sees the BLACK 1970 DODGE
CHALLENGER coming toward the CLUB.

                                        CUT TO:

INT. BLACK 1970 DODGE CHALLENGER - MOMENTS LATER

MICHAEL is hauling ass in his BLACK 1970 DODGE CHALLENGER,
while smoking a joint; he straps on his seat-belt and cuts
off the Mozart music. He is headed straight toward AGENT
WHITE and his HENCHMEN...

                    MICHAEL
                 (putting on his
                  seatbelt)
          There you are, you motherfucker!!!

MICHAEL hits his joint a couple of more times and then puts
it out.

                                        CUT TO:

EXT. MIAMI CLUB - MOMENTS LATER

WHITE knows it's MICHAEL...

WHITE is scared shitless, and is practically speechless.

                    AGENT WHITE
          Holy shit!!!

WHITE throws down the phone and scrambles into the CLUB. The
GOON just stands there, thinking it's someone trying to show
off.

EXT. MIAMI CLUB - CONTINUOUS

WHITE'S phone is on the ground...

                    AGENT ORANGE
               (through the phone)
          Hello?!?!

                                        CUT TO:

INT. BLACK 1970 DODGE CHALLENGER - CONTINUOUS

MICHAEL floors it. He is going just about as fast as he can.
The CAR sounds like a pack of roaring Lions...

                                        CUT TO:

MICHAEL runs over the GOON standing outside of the CLUB,
crushing him with the BLACK 1970 DODGE CHALLENGER, and
MICHAEL crashes the CAR into the CLUB at full speed, causing
catastrophic damage...

                                        CUT TO:

INT. MIAMI CLUB - MOMENTS LATER

AGENT WHITE is utterly terrified by MICHAEL'S epic
entrance...

                    AGENT WHITE
               (yelling to all
                his HENCHMEN)
          Kill whoever-the-fuck gets out of
          that CAR!

AGENT WHITE hides...

All the HENCHMEN are stunned and confused...

                              CUT TO:

INT. MIAMI CLUB - CONTINUOUS

MICHAEL immediately gets out of his CAR with M-16 in-hand,
prepared to shoot anything that moves.

MICHAEL'S CAR is barely damaged. It is nearly indestructible
CAR; MICHAEL built it that way.

                              CUT TO:

Three HENCHMEN appear with guns drawn. They spray plenty of
bullets at MICHAEL.

MICHAEL ducks down behind his CAR. He then rises up, aiming
tactically at the targets, and he shoots each of the three
HENCHMEN in both of their knees, with terrific accuracy,
only using six bullets from his M-16...

MICHAEL has a tactical-strap for his M-16 that goes across
his chest and extends to his back. He straps the M-16 to his
back.

MICHAEL then slowly walks up to the three HENCHMEN...

                              CUT TO:

MICHAEL pulls out his 9MM.

                    HENCHMAN #1
                (grabbing leg)
          Ah!!!

The three HENCHMEN are in great agony.

                    HENCHMAN #2
          Don't kill me, man, don't kill me!
          I just work for them!

                    HENCHMAN #3
                (grabbing leg)
          Ah!!!

MICHAEL does not respond to the HENCHMAN...

MICHAEL is consumed by vengeance...

He, with no hesitation, shoots all 3 HENCHMEN in the head
with his 9MM.

He then puts the pistol back in the holster...

MICHAEL is looking for AGENT WHITE...

CUT TO:

MICHAEL walks slowly through the CLUB.

Four more HENCHMEN run toward MICHAEL, and they surround him. The four HENCHMEN are unarmed.

MICHAEL does not want to use his firearm against them. Rather, he wants to fight them. He wants to get his blood pumping...

Only those 4 HENCHMEN remain in the CLUB...

AGENT WHITE is still hiding...

CUT TO:

The four remaining HENCHMEN attack MICHAEL...

MICHAEL is a supremely skilled fighter. He actually trained special-forces in the military, and has a very formidable fighting-style.

MICHAEL single-handedly holds their punches off...

MICHAEL then elbows HENCHMAN#4, momentarily incapacitating him; subsequently, MICHAEL punches him in the face so hard that the man's face breaks and caves in. HENCHMAN#4 is dead.

MICHAEL then kicks HENCHMAN#5 directly in the throat, crushing his wind-pipe; The HENCHMAN gasps for air, and dies immediately...

HENCHMEN#6 takes a swing at MICHAEL...

MICHAEL pulls a knife, grabs HENCHMAN #6 by the neck and stabs him through the chin into the brain.

We can see the blade shining in the man's mouth. The HENCHMAN collapses.

Only one HENCHMAN remains...

MICHAEL runs up to HENCHMAN#7 and grabs him by the neck, picking him up off his feet...

MICHAEL squeezes the HENCHMAN'S neck with great strength, and breaks his neck with ease. The HENCHMAN'S eyes roll into the back of his head and he abruptly dies.

CUT TO:

AGENT WHITE appears from behind the bar with his hands up.
He is unarmed.

                    AGENT WHITE
          MIKEY, listen, okay, just
          listen!!!

WHITE has the fear of GOD in him.

                    AGENT WHITE
          I'm unarmed. I'll tell you exactly
          where ORANGE is--we can resolve
          this.

The 7 HENCHMEN in the CLUB are dead; none are left to
protect AGENT WHITE.

MICHAEL slowly walks up to WHITE, intimidating him...

                    MICHAEL
          Do you want to know what I've
          learned, CARL?

WHITE is terrified, because he knows MICHAEL is going to
kill him.

MICHAEL pulls out a fat joint from out of nowhere. He lights
the joint.

                    MICHAEL
               (puffing the joint)
          Pot is God's greatest creation. We
          humans are nothing in comparison
          to this plant...
               (tokes his joint)
          ...They say humanity is God's
          greatest creation, but that's
          bullshit. This plant is God's
          greatest creation...
               (hits the joint
                several more
                times)
          ...It could cure the planet and
          heal the nations. It could fix the
          human condition. This plant was
          invented to bring peace to the
          earth. It's people who stop the
          world from having the peace it so
          rightfully deserves. You know what
          I mean, WHITE?

                    AGENT WHITE
          Y-y-yeah, MICHAEL. I guess so.

                    MICHAEL
          Here you go, CARL, this should
          calm you down a little-bit.

WHITE is nervous and shaking in fear.

MICHAEL, ironically enough, gestures to WHITE to hit the
joint.

                    AGENT WHITE
          W-w-why are y-you gonna let me hit
          that?--

When WHITE goes to grab the joint, MICHAEL jerks it back
away from him. He is toying with AGENT WHITE.

                    MICHAEL
          --Well, you're the only one that's
          alive in here. But, really, you
          seem like you could use a toke...
                    (hits the joint
                     two more times)
          ...Plus, I don't feel like smoking
          this by myself, and I'm smoking
          right now, regardless.

                                        CUT TO:

MICHAEL finally hands AGENT WHITE the joint...

WHITE takes the joint, but he is totally confused...

WHITE hits the joint several times very hard; he's almost
like a caught criminal, during an interrogation, smoking a
cigarette the cops have offered him.

                    MICHAEL
          Now, you may proceed with what you
          were going to tell me about
          ORANGE...when is he coming back?
          You tell me these things that I
          need to know, and perhaps, just
          perhaps, I will make this easier
          on you than I did on SMITH.

                    AGENT WHITE
          Y-y-you got to SMITH?

                    MICHAEL
          Damn, CARL, I thought you already
          knew that...

After hearing that MICHAEL has already killed AGENT SMITH,
AGENT WHITE becomes distraught.

WHITE complies with MICHAEL.

                    AGENT WHITE
          Holy Shit, all right! He'll be
          back tonight, a few hours from
          now. I swear! He'll be at his
          HOTEL!

                    MICHAEL
          --How many?--

WHITE hits the joint almost like a crack-head to a
crack-pipe.

                    AGENT WHITE
          --How many what?--

MICHAEL slaps AGENT WHITE upside the head really hard...

                    MICHAEL
          --How many men will be there,
          CARL? Don't play stupid!

                    AGENT WHITE
          I don't know, MIKEY! 30, 40? I
          don't fucking know! You know he
          practically owns the damn thing!
          He's got the whole building bought
          and paid for, cameras on every
          floor! What are you gonna do?! You
          can't beat that, MIKEY! You go in
          there, and he'll have his guys
          kill you in a split-second!

                    MICHAEL
                 (seemingly
                 careless)
          Thank you for the information,
          WHITE. Now, hit the joint again
          and pass it.

WHITE hits the joint one last good time and then passes it
to MICHAEL quite fearfully.

MICHAEL snatches the joint from WHITE...

                              CUT TO:

MICHAEL tokes on the joint till it's burning his
finger-tips, then he proceeds to eat the roach and burp
smoke...

                    AGENT WHITE
          You ain't gonna kill me???

                    MICHAEL
          Kill you? Not right now. I got
          something special planned for
          you...

                    AGENT WHITE
          Ah, shit...

MICHAEL punches WHITE in the face with great force knocking
him out. MICHAEL puts AGENT WHITE in the trunk of the BLACK
1970 DODGE CHALLENGER, backs the CAR out of the CLUB and
takes off...

MICHAEL'S CAR is fixed up; interior and exterior. It is
completely upgraded and customized. It's practically a
'Bat-mobile'...

MICHAEL has kidnapped AGENT WHITE...

AGENT ORANGE doesn't know what has happened at his CLUB. He
has no idea that MICHAEL has WHITE. He has no clue that
MICHAEL knows where he'll be...

AGENT ORANGE is unaware that MICHAEL TEDESCO is coming for
him...

                              CUT TO:

EXT. MIAMI AIRPORT - NIGHT

ORANGE gets off of his private-jet. He is wearing a business
suit with his orange tie. He enters his VEHICLE: A ORANGE
LIMOUSINE...

                              CUT TO:

INT. ORANGE'S CAR - MOMENTS LATER

                    AGENT ORANGE
                (to his DRIVER)
          Get me to the fucking CLUB! NOW!!!

                    DRIVER
                 (scrambling)
              Yes, Sir, Boss!

The DRIVER drives away from the MIAMI AIRPORT in a hurry at
ORANGE'S demand.

                                          CUT TO:

INT. ORANGE'S CAR - LATER

The DRIVER and ORANGE pull up near the CLUB.

AGENT ORANGE inspects the CLUB from inside of his ORANGE
LIMOUSINE.

There are police all over the place...

ORANGE sees the damage and is shocked...

                    AGENT ORANGE
                 (soliloquy)
              What the fuck?!

                                          CUT TO:

The DRIVER begins heading toward the scene and the police...

                                          CUT TO:

                    AGENT ORANGE
                 (snorting coke)
              What the fuck?! Why are you
              driving toward them?! There are
              POLICE everywhere! Turn around and
              get me to the HOTEL, you idiot!

                    DRIVER
                 (petrified)
              You got it, Boss!

The DRIVER turns the ORANGE LIMOUSINE around, and proceeds
to take AGENT ORANGE to the HOTEL...

AGENT ORANGE is heading right into MICHAEL'S trap...

                                          CUT TO:

EXT. ORANGE'S CAR - MOMENTS LATER

AGENT ORANGE gets out of his ORANGE LIMOUSINE and proceeds
to enter his HOTEL.

THE DRIVER is just sitting in the ORANGE LIMOUSINE outside
of the HOTEL.

As soon as AGENT ORANGE enters the HOTEL, MICHAEL taps on
the driver-side window of the ORANGE LIMOUSINE. THE DRIVER
stupidly rolls down the window.

MICHAEL reaches in the ORANGE LIMOUSINE with terrifying
quickness and snaps THE DRIVER'S neck like a chicken-bone.

                              CUT TO:

INT. ORANGE'S HOTEL - CONTINUOUS

AGENT ORANGE walks through the revolving-door of his HOTEL,
pissed off at the world. ORANGE'S HOTEL is first-class, and
it is also one of his base of operations; the HOTEL has
ORANGE and white checkered-flooring...

AGENT ORANGE is on the phone, raving like a lunatic...

                    AGENT ORANGE
                 (into the phone
                 with roaring
                 command)
          Get every able body we got, come
          here, right fucking now! Find out
          what the fuck has happened to
          WHITE! And, where the fuck is
          SMITH?!

There are about 18 GOONS in the HOTEL lobby...

ORANGE begins to walk up the stairs. He is still ranting
into the phone. Subsequently, about 40 more GOONS come from
the rooms of the HOTEL and run down the stairs as if they
are preparing for a small war.

                    AGENT ORANGE
                 (yelling at the
                 top of his lungs
                 into the phone)
          I don't care if you have to look
          under every crevasse, pebble,
          every piece of dirt...
                 (snorts coke)
          ...You ask every snitch we got,
          you ask every person on the
                    (MORE)

                    AGENT ORANGE (cont'd)
          streets!!! I want to know who
          destroyed my CLUB! I want to know
          how! And, I want to know now!

The revolving-door of the HOTEL begins to spin, and AGENT
WHITE enters. WHITE has duck-tape on his mouth and his hands
are tied behind his back.

                    AGENT WHITE
               (yelling through
               the duck-tape)
          Mmm! Mmm! Mmm!

WHITE falls to his knees. Underneath his shirt it seems as
if his chest is bulging.

                    AGENT ORANGE
          CARL?! What the hell's happened to
          you?! Who did this?!
               (points to one of
               the GOONS)
          You! Get that tape off of his face
          and untie his hands...
               (stares down
               WHITE'S bulging
               chest)
          ...CARL, what the fuck is wrong
          with your chest?!

The GOON approaches WHITE, and proceeds to take the tape off
of his face.

WHITE immediately shouts....

                    AGENT WHITE
               (shouting)
          It's a BOMB!!!

We here a "beep. beep."

WHITE, the GOON, and 29 other GOONS are killed as WHITE'S
chest is covered with C4 and Semtex explosives that go off.
The blast sends limbs and heads across the HOTEL lobby; the
loudness of the blast is tremendous.

Fire rushes out of the HOTEL entrance and many of the
windows as the explosion transpires; a lot of the HOTEL
windows shatter, as does the revolving-door glass...

                    AGENT ORANGE
               (shocked, dodging
               limbs)
          Holy Fuck!!!
                    (MORE)

                    AGENT ORANGE (cont'd)
                   (panicked, ducking)
          He's here.

There is no sprinkler-system in the HOTEL; AGENT ORANGE had
the sprinkler-system removed from the place. There are many
patches of flames all around the HOTEL lobby, but the fire
does not spread and the HOTEL itself does not catch on fire.

                                        CUT TO:

EXT. ORANGE'S HOTEL - CONTINUOUS

MICHAEL has a SPAS-12-gauge shotgun in his hands, a knife in
a sheath on his waist, a G-18 pistol in his holster on his
side, and a M-16 strapped to his back. He readies himself...

He is walking very fast, and very tenaciously...

MICHAEL points his shotgun and enters the HOTEL through the
shattered revolving-door, ready to kill.

                                        CUT TO:

INT. ORANGE'S HOTEL - MOMENTS LATER

There are 28 GOONS left in ORANGE'S crew. Most of them are
disorientated from the blast...

The other GOONS that AGENT ORANGE called for will not
arrive. They won't arrive because the cops have blocked off
the surrounding areas around the HOTEL, preventing any
traffic from flowing toward or from ORANGE'S HOTEL...

                                        CUT TO:

INT. ORANGE'S HOTEL - CONTINUOUS

MICHAEL runs into the HOTEL quite swiftly. He shoots six
GOONS with his SPAS-12-gauge shotgun, sending them flying in
the air; the GOONS die...

MICHAEL throws his shotgun down on the floor...

MICHAEL sprints and then rolls on the ground,
military-style. He pulls his G-18 pistol, gets into a crouch
position and shoots three more GOONS.

MICHAEL then stands up and starts running horizontally:

running and gunning. He kills five more GOONS.

His accuracy is superb. Rather than spraying and praying, he is spraying and massacring.

CUT TO:

MICHAEL puts his G-18 pistol back in the holster...

He runs up to another GOON, quickly pulls his knife, and stabs the GOON in the neck; blood sprays everywhere.

MICHAEL then, in one quick motion, runs up to seven more GOONS and uses unique stabbing techniques; MICHAEL stabs and slices the GOONS with tremendous quickness...

The GOONS immediately fall to the ground screaming in pain.

The GOONS start gasping for air and gargling their own blood. They die very painfully.

MICHAEL puts his knife back in the sheath.

CUT TO:

The remaining 6 GOONS shoot at MICHAEL. MICHAEL takes cover behind a column, pulls the pin on a flash-bang grenade and throws it...

The flash-bang grenade explodes and stuns the remaining GOONS.

MICHAEL pulls his M-16 from off his back and prepares to shoot. He takes a low-stance, targets the 6 GOONS and knocks them down like bottles at a shooting range. MICHAEL shoots each of the GOONS in their left-knee-cap.

They're still alive. The GOONS are grabbing their left legs and yelling in pain. MICHAEL walks up to each remaining GOON, and shoots each one in the head with his rifle. The yells cease...

Revenge is Blind.

CUT TO:

MICHAEL has killed all of ORANGE'S available crew. It's now just AGENT ORANGE and MICHAEL.

MICHAEL does not want to shoot ORANGE and end it so fast. He wants to brutally beat ORANGE. He wants to kill him with his bare-hands. But, he knows he cannot...

MICHAEL'S soul, and the power feeding his rage are leaving him and he knows it.

CUT TO:

EXPOSITION:

AGENT ORANGE is unafraid of MICHAEL, vice-versa...

AGENT ORANGE, like MICHAEL, is also a trained killer.

AGENT ORANGE, AGENT WHITE, and AGENT SMITH worked with the CIA, prior to joining the DEA; they were operatives. AGENT ORANGE was a very skilled "cleaner"/assassin for the CIA and he was also the handler of AGENT WHITE and AGENT SMITH.

AGENT ORANGE left the CIA for the DEA, and WHITE and SMITH followed him to the DEA. They always follow AGENT ORANGE'S lead...

After joining The DEA, AGENT ORANGE, AGENT WHITE, and AGENT SMITH began extorting from marijuana-dealers and marijuana-farmers. The AGENTS take tons of pot and cash from farmers and dealers; those they cannot extort from, they kill.

ORANGE, SMITH, and WHITE ultimately left The DEA and went Renegade. The RENEGADE AGENTS attacked and robbed The DEA BUILDING in 2012. The AGENT'S attack on The DEA BUILDING greatly hurt The Drug Enforcement Agency.

MICHAEL dealt with AGENT ORANGE for quite a period of time as the Renegade AGENT coerced him to cultivate marijuana for his operation. ORANGE threatened to hurt MICHAEL and his family if he didn't comply.

MICHAEL, wanting to shed the tyrannical ORANGE from his life, severed ties with the monstrous AGENT and moved to WEWAHITCHKA.

MICHAEL moved to WEWAHITCHKA because it is about as low-key as he could get and he wanted to elude AGENT ORANGE while still remaining close to his customers. MICHAEL figured if he moved to the woods of Northwest FLORIDA, then ORANGE wouldn't find him. MICHAEL was mistaken; AGENT ORANGE could find Jimmy Hoffa...

AGENT ORANGE eventually found out MICHAEL'S whereabouts after 4 years of looking. After finding MICHAEL'S location, AGENT ORANGE gathered WHITE and SMITH, and they went to assassinate MICHAEL and his family...

CUT TO:

EXT. ORANGE'S HOTEL - CONTINUOUS

The POLICE start to surround the HOTEL, because they heard
the explosion.

Although they've surrounded it, they do not enter: 1.
Because it's ORANGE'S HOTEL 2. ORANGE is practically
untouchable 3. Because the police suspect that there may be
other explosives in the building.

                                        CUT TO:

DETECTIVE MARSHALL finally arrives at the scene of CHAOS.

                                        CUT TO:

INT. ORANGE'S HOTEL - MOMENTS LATER

AGENT ORANGE slowly walks down the HOTEL stairs. MICHAEL
puts his weapons on the floor; he drops his M-16 and he
throws his knife and G-18 pistol down...

                    AGENT ORANGE
                  (with a vile tone)
             MICHAEL, you're back from the
             dead, huh? Like Lazarus himself.
             You've made a grave mistake coming
             here tonight. I killed you once, I
             guess I'll just have to kill you
             again so you can rest in peace
             with your family, huh? To be
             honest, I actually enjoyed killing
             them. Typically, I don't enjoy
             killing women and children, but
             this was an exception. I
             thoroughly enjoyed it, MICHAEL.

                    MICHAEL
                  (in tremendous
                   pain)
             This ends now.

ORANGE gets to the bottom of the steps. MICHAEL and AGENT
ORANGE proceed to fight...

AGENT ORANGE swings on MICHAEL, but MICHAEL catches his fist
mid-way and kicks ORANGE directly in the chest.

                                        CUT TO:

MICHAEL proceeds to hit ORANGE several times within a matter
of seconds: He hits his body, face, knees, arms, and neck

with tenacious and speedy elbows, kicks, and punches...

MICHAEL is bleeding very badly from the gun-shot wounds and the knife wound that ORANGE gave him. His soul is struggling to cling to the world of the living.

MICHAEL grabs AGENT ORANGE by his orange tie and hits the AGENT with a strong uppercut. ORANGE takes the hit, and starts laughing with a sinister tone.

MICHAEL barely hurt ORANGE and has drained himself of all his remaining energy.

AGENT ORANGE punches MICHAEL in the face and knocks him backward.

ORANGE sprints toward MICHAEL, and delivers an elbow directly to his face, laughing mercilessly. AGENT ORANGE'S mouth is full of blood.

The masochistic son-of-a-bitch spits blood right in MICHAEL'S face.

                                        CUT TO:

ORANGE slams MICHAEL against the wall, and knees him multiple times in the stomach.

ORANGE is punching and kicking the hell out of MICHAEL.

MICHAEL does not retaliate, as he is spiritually and physically exhausted. All he wants is to see his family.

MICHAEL wants to die. If he kills ORANGE, he will then have nothing to live for. He only lived for his family until Death took them from him. Now, Death is upon MICHAEL.

MICHAEL wants to join MARIA, APRIL, and little MIKEY. He lets ORANGE beat him in the body until he simply falls down.

MICHAEL is dying. He is mostly dying from his loss...

AGENT ORANGE sucker-punches MICHAEL one last time.

                                        CUT TO:

ORANGE pulls a knife; the knife has a blade composed of Chromium and Titanium...

                    AGENT ORANGE
            MICHAEL, Death always comes too
            early or too late.

AGENT ORANGE stabs MICHAEL, through his jacket and his bullet-proof vest, in the right side of his chest. AGENT ORANGE stabs MICHAEL so hard that it punctures his right-lung...

                                        CUT TO:

MICHAEL gasps and collapses against the wall. He slides into a sitting-position...

He is leaking blood.

                    AGENT ORANGE
            Pathetic...
                (spits on MICHAEL)
            ...You'll not have your Revenge
            today, my friend.

MICHAEL is sitting against the wall, almost lifeless...

He manages to pull the knife from his chest, and blood pours from the wound. Yet, the blood looks like water.

AGENT ORANGE leaves MICHAEL be...

AGENT ORANGE fixes his orange tie; he has blood all over it.

AGENT ORANGE then turns to MICHAEL, smiles, and puts his hands up.

                    AGENT ORANGE
                (smiling)
            I'll see ya on the other side,
            MIKEY...

ORANGE starts to exit the HOTEL with his hands held high...

MICHAEL is incapacitated.

AGENT ORANGE knows his operation is over, but he is prepared to take on the role of snitch and rat out his connections in exchange for a lighter sentence...

AGENT ORANGE, despite all the CHAOS he has caused, knows he'll be out of incarceration in a short amount of time.

DETECTIVE MARSHALL knows that MICHAEL is innocent, and that ORANGE is the one responsible for killing MICHAEL'S family...

MARSHALL simply wants to find justice for little MIKEY, APRIL, and MARIA by apprehending ORANGE, and getting whatever charges he can against him.

                                        CUT TO:

EXT. ORANGE'S HOTEL - MOMENTS LATER

AGENT ORANGE walks outside with his hands up. The POLICE
start shouting all-together: "HANDS UP ON YOUR HEAD, FACE ON
THE GROUND!"

                                        CUT TO:

ORANGE complies and lies face-down with his hands on his
head. DETECTIVE MARSHALL runs toward AGENT ORANGE...

                    POLICE SERGEANT
             DETECTIVE, what the hell are you
             doing?! Halt!

DETECTIVE MARSHALL ignores the SERGEANT, and continues
toward ORANGE.

Some of the other OFFICERS attempt to stop MARSHALL, but
he's too quick. The OFFICERS try to follow MARSHALL, only to
be stopped by the SERGEANT.

                    POLICE SERGEANT
                 (holding back the
                  officers)
             Stand down, let MARSHALL handle
             it!

AGENT ORANGE rolls over onto his back.

                    DETECTIVE MARSHALL
                 (pointing his
                  weapon at AGENT
                  ORANGE)
             ORANGE! Don't you fucking move!

                    AGENT ORANGE
                 (vicious)
             Why so aggressive, DETECTIVE? You
             haven't even read me my rights. Go
             ahead, arrest me. I'll give up a
             few names, serve a little time,
             and I'll be out so quickly, it'll
             make your fucking head spin, my
             friend. All while you'll be
             pushing papers in Alaska till I
             find you, and gut you. Think
             before you act, DETECTIVE...
                 (with a vile tone)
             I got your family, I'll get you
                      (MORE)

AGENT ORANGE (cont'd)
        too...

                                          CUT TO:

MARSHALL is shocked by ORANGE'S words; the DETECTIVE takes a couple steps back in disbelief...

                    DETECTIVE MARSHALL
                         (shocked)
                    W-w-what'd you say, you
                    son-of-a-bitch?

MARSHALL has been searching for the killer of his family for years. He has prayed. He has cried. He has grieved every single day they've been gone. DETECTIVE MARSHALL has spent many days and nights thinking of what he would do to the person who took his family from him...

                    AGENT ORANGE
                         (grinning)
                    You heard me, MARSHALL. You heard
                    me. Your wife screamed before I
                    shot her. However, your children
                    barely made a peep before I killed
                    them. I slit their throats so
                    fast, and they bled so slow...

                                          CUT TO:

MARSHALL is devastated after hearing AGENT ORANGE'S dark confession. The DETECTIVE now has fire in his eyes.

However, DETECTIVE MARSHALL refrains from harming AGENT ORANGE.

The DETECTIVE reads AGENT ORANGE his rights: "You have the right to remain silent..."

MARSHALL is a man of the law, and he wants justice to be done, but not by his own hands...

DETECTIVE MARSHALL flips AGENT ORANGE over onto his stomach and handcuffs him. MARSHALL turns toward the HOTEL with great awareness. The DETECTIVE knows that MICHAEL TEDESCO is in there. He slowly walks into the HOTEL with his gun in-hand.

                                          CUT TO:

INT. ORANGE'S HOTEL - MOMENTS LATER

MICHAEL is lying down against the wall. He is on the verge
of Death...

MICHAEL sees MARSHALL walking toward him with his weapon
pointed...

MICHAEL then blinks, and suddenly he sees his FAMILY as well
as a heavenly light...

                    DETECTIVE MARSHALL
                  (with authority)
            TEDESECO, freeze! Put your hands
            up and put your face on the
            ground, now!

                       MICHAEL
                  (eyes wide and
                   smiling)
            MARIA, APRIL, MIKEY...I'm with you
            n--

MICHAEL takes his last breath with a smile on his face.

MICHAEL is now dead.

MARSHALL searches MICHAEL, and he finds something in his
jacket-pocket...

The List...

The List reads: 1. RAY SMITH, 2. CARL WHITE, 3. KIMBO
ORANGE. It has MICHAEL'S blood on it, yet it is still
readable.

MARSHALL sees that that SMITH'S and WHITE'S names are
crossed out on The List. It gives him a sense anger to see
that ORANGE'S name won't be crossed out and that MICHAEL
didn't get the justice he sought.

MARSHALL is absolutely disgusted by the fact that ORANGE is
the one that killed his wife and children, and he is filled
with rage knowing that ORANGE also murdered MICHAEL'S
family.

A shift occurs in MARSHALL. He has a revelation.

Lightning strikes and thunder roars outside of the HOTEL...

                                        CUT TO:

DETECTIVE MARSHALL exits the HOTEL...

                              CUT TO:

EXT. ORANGE'S HOTEL - MOMENTS LATER

DETECTIVE MARSHALL proceeds to walk up to AGENT ORANGE...

                              CUT TO:

AGENT ORANGE is still lying on the ground, handcuffed. He is
lying on his back, on top of his cuffed hands. The other
policemen are still standing back and they do not move
toward AGENT ORANGE and DETECTIVE MARSHALL.

MARSHALL stands over AGENT ORANGE.

                    AGENT ORANGE
                 (condescending)
          Well, you gonna take me in,
          MARSHALL, like a good
          little-piggie?

                    DETECTIVE MARSHALL
                 (points his pistol
                  at AGENT ORANGE)
          I'm not a cop anymore.

MARSHALL unloads a full clip into AGENT ORANGE...

                              CUT TO:

ORANGE takes his last breath and succumbs to Death...

Rain starts pouring from the night-sky.

                              CUT TO:

The police immediately react. Most of the cops are yelling
indistinctly.

Some of the cops shout: "DROP IT, MARSHALL!"

CHAOS has consumed the scene.

MARSHALL complies. He drops the smoking-gun, and puts his
hands in the air, standing as still as a statue.

He has blood on his hands...

He also has a vengeful smirk on his face.

The police slowly swarm in on MARSHALL with their guns
pointed at him.

The rain falls harder. It is torrential. The Heavens cry joyous tears at the sight of Justice...

                                        SLOWLY PAN OUT/SKY
                                        VIEW

                                        CUT TO BLACK:

                                        TITLE APPEARANCE:
                                        ORGANIZED CHAOS

                        THE END